# Manifestation Diaries

*Proven Techniques for Manifesting Your Dreams*

**VOLUME 1**

**INTERNATIONAL COUNCIL OF AUTHORS**
**BY**
**INSPIRING JATIN**

Chennai • Bangalore

CLEVER FOX PUBLISHING
Chennai, India

Published by CLEVER FOX PUBLISHING 2025
Copyright © International Council of Authors by Inspiring Jatin 2025

All Rights Reserved.
ISBN: 978-93-67071-58-8

This book has been published with all reasonable efforts taken to make the material error-free after the consent of the author. No part of this book shall be used, reproduced in any manner whatsoever without written permission from the author, except in the case of brief quotations embodied in critical articles and reviews.

The Author of this book is solely responsible and liable for its content including but not limited to the views, representations, descriptions, statements, information, opinions and references ["Content"]. The Content of this book shall not constitute or be construed or deemed to reflect the opinion or expression of the Publisher or Editor. Neither the Publisher nor Editor endorse or approve the Content of this book or guarantee the reliability, accuracy or completeness of the Content published herein and do not make any representations or warranties of any kind, express or implied, including but not limited to the implied warranties of merchantability, fitness for a particular purpose. The Publisher and Editor shall not be liable whatsoever for any errors, omissions, whether such errors or omissions result from negligence, accident, or any other cause or claims for loss or damages of any kind, including without limitation, indirect or consequential loss or damage arising out of use, inability to use, or about the reliability, accuracy or sufficiency of the information contained in this book.

# CONTENTS

Introduction .................................................................vii
By Inspiring Jatin

1. Surya's Manifestations' Journey ...............................1
By N. Surya Prakash

2. The Dance of Manifestation .......................................7
By Shree Shambav

3. Manifesting the Unseen ...........................................13
By Nita Rathod

4. Hopelessness to Hopefulness: My Motherhood
Manifestation Journey .............................................19
By Maneesha Singh

5. Miracles Unfold: Manifesting Land, Home, And
Bestseller Status ......................................................25
By Dr. Deepa Didddi

6. My Manifestation Journey: From Self Doubt,
Self Hate, and Ignorant Student to A Confident,
Lovable, Familiar Doctor .........................................31
By Dr Sathya Priyanka

## Contents

7. The Power of Manifestation: A Journey to Dream Fulfilment ..................39
   By Thandavarayan M.

8. Healing Through Manifestation: My Journey to Wellness and Empowerment .................47
   By Dr. Pratibhaa Borade

9. Manifesting the Yogic Way .................53
   By Suchita Sanjay

10. Manifesting Miracles: How I Met the President of India 2023 .................59
    By Maino Murmu

11. From Vision To Reality: How I Built The Life I Always Envisioned .................65
    By Monika Rai

12. From Desperation to Manifestation: A Journey of Transformation .................71
    – By Bajan Bopanna

13. Manifesting Magic .................77
    By Anu Malik Garg

14. From Aspiration to Achievement: A Manifestation Journey .................83
    By Suryanarayana S.V.

15. From Trauma to Transformation: A Journey of Self-Discovery .................89
    By Dr. Gaveshana Shrotriya

**16.** Manifesting the Life You Desire: A Personal Journey of Belief and Transformation......................95
By Sushil Grover

**17.** The Secret Ingredient That Helped Me Manifest In Seconds! ..........................................................101
By Juhi Damodar

**18.** From Humble Beginnings to Global Success: My Manifestation Journey ......................................105
By Sujoy Chowdhury

**19.** A Pen and A Vision ................................................111
By Japjot Kang

**20.** Manifestation Gone Wrong....................................117
By Anshu Joshi Singh

**21.** Manifesting Wholeness: A Journey of Healing and Transformation...............................................123
By Vijay Singla

**22.** From Dreams To Best Sellers................................129
By Rashmi K.

**23.** The Dream That Refused to Die ............................135
By Ruchika Bhasker

**24.** Baking my dream into a reality .............................141
By Madhuri Premnath

**25.** From Fear to Miracles: A Journey of Faith, Healing, and Manifestation ....................................147
By Swati Sharrma

## Contents

**26.** The Power of My "Why" ........................................... 153
By Tayyaba Fatima

**27.** From Chaos to Clarity: Manifesting My Life
Purpose .................................................................. 159
By Anand Iyer

**28.** Manifestations, The Universe Stamping ................. 165
By Nazneen Zeeshan Ali

**29.** The Power of Intention: Setting the Foundation
for My Manifestation Journey ................................ 171
By Jyoti KR Aroraa

**30.** Frozen Fury and Unshaken Spirit .......................... 177
By Rupali Mukherjee

**31.** Magic Canvas of a Schoolgirl: A Life Well-Lived .... 185
By Swapnil Roy 'Soultinker

Conclusion: Embracing the Power of
Manifestation ........................................................ 191
Join the Movement: Share Your Manifestation
Goals! .................................................................... 195
Your Story Deserves to Be Told—Become a
Self Published Author! .......................................... 197

# INTRODUCTION: TRANSFORMING DREAMS INTO REALITY

$\mathcal{D}$eep within each individual lies an immense reservoir of potential—a force that, when harnessed effectively, can bring dreams to life. My own journey toward understanding and embracing this extraordinary power often referred to as "manifestation," began years ago, though I had no idea then that it would shape the course of my life so profoundly.

## Discovering Manifestation

My first brush with manifestation happened somewhat incidentally. I watched the documentary *The Secret* while working in the corporate sector, unaware of the depth of its teachings. At that time, the concept seemed abstract and too good to be true—something I neither practiced nor fully understood.

Years later, while pursuing my certification as a life coach, the concept resurfaced through a mentor who reintroduced me to the law of attraction. This time, I paid attention. Slowly, I began exploring the principles and integrating them into my life.

A pivotal moment came during a coaching assignment that required me to set a tangible goal. I wrote down my aspiration: to become an author by June 2020. At the time, it felt like just another exercise, but it turned out to be a manifestation in action. By May 31, 2020, despite the challenges posed by a global pandemic, my manuscript was complete. That milestone not only affirmed my belief in manifestation but also solidified my understanding of how powerful a focused mind and intentional action can be.

This realization transformed my perspective. I came to understand that when thoughts, emotions, and actions align toward a clear vision, the universe conspires to make it happen.

Introduction: Transforming Dreams Into Reality

## A Defining Moment: The Birth of ICA

The idea for the International Council of Authors (ICA) was sparked by an unforgettable experience. I had the privilege of participating in a Guinness World Record attempt as part of a group of speakers representing India. This event was life-changing, revealing the strength of collaboration and the impact of pursuing a common goal.

That experience planted the seeds of the ICA. I envisioned a community that would support authors in their creative journeys, empowering them to achieve incredible milestones. The ICA has since evolved into much more than a writers' platform; it is a dynamic community that fosters growth, celebrates accomplishments, and provides unique opportunities for authors to leave a mark on the world.

Through initiatives such as anthologies, publishing events, and world record attempts, the ICA has become a beacon of support and inspiration for both new and seasoned authors.

## Why Focus on Manifestation?

Manifestation is not just a practice; it is a way of life. It enables individuals to bring their thoughts and aspirations into reality by aligning their inner and outer worlds. Choosing "manifestation" as the theme for this anthology felt like a natural extension of my own journey and belief in its transformative power.

Over the years, I've witnessed how manifestation changes lives—mine and those of countless others. From achieving personal goals to helping clients unlock their potential, the consistent truth is that when we believe in a vision and take aligned action, the universe responds.

This anthology is a tribute to that truth. It features real-life stories of resilience, courage, and triumph. Each chapter encapsulates the remarkable power of manifestation, offering readers a glimpse into how individuals from diverse backgrounds have realized their dreams.

## Embracing Happiness as a Life Coach

For me, happiness is the freedom to live authentically without fear—whether it's the fear of judgment, failure, or the unknown. My path to becoming a life coach was deeply personal, marked by struggles with limiting beliefs that hindered my growth in many areas of life.

Through self-discovery and determination, I transformed my outlook and resolved to help others do the same. My coaching philosophy revolves around empowering individuals to overcome obstacles, release negativity, and create lives filled with purpose, joy, and fulfilment.

Writing plays a crucial role in this process. It offers a unique way to reflect, heal, and create. For many, the act of becoming an author is life-changing—it's a journey of self-expression and personal growth.

## The Rewards of Authorship

Writing a book is one of the most rewarding pursuits. It allows individuals to:

- **Achieve Tangible Goals**: There's a profound sense of accomplishment in holding your published work in your hands.
- **Foster Growth**: Writing encourages introspection and discipline, leading to personal transformation.
- **Leave a Legacy**: A book immortalizes your thoughts and ideas, creating a lasting impact.
- **Build Connections**: Sharing your story can resonate with readers and form meaningful bonds.

Publishing also elevates one's credibility. Being an author opens doors to new opportunities such as public speaking, media exposure, and collaborations, while also establishing you as a thought leader in your field. My journey as an author has been instrumental in building trust and expanding my reach as a coach.

Introduction: Transforming Dreams Into Reality

## The Purpose Behind This Anthology

This anthology is more than just a collection of stories. It represents my dream of creating a ripple effect of positivity and success. Through the ICA, I aim to inspire individuals to recognize and unlock their potential, share their unique wisdom, and make a lasting impact.

The theme of manifestation perfectly aligns with this mission. It resonates universally, offering readers practical insights, motivation, and inspiration. Each story in this anthology serves as a blueprint for success, providing hope and encouragement to anyone striving to bring their dreams to life.

## A Personal Message to Readers

To everyone holding this book, know that it isn't a coincidence that you've come across it. The stories you'll read are filled with lessons, triumphs, and inspiration, proving that dreams can indeed become reality.

If these authors have succeeded in manifesting their goals, so can you. Manifestation is not a secret limited to a select few; it is a gift available to anyone willing to believe, act, and persevere.

Welcome to a journey of transformation, where dreams are not just imagined but realized. Welcome to the limitless power of manifestation.

# SURYA'S MANIFESTATIONS' JOURNEY

## BY N. SURYA PRAKASH

$\mathcal{W}$hen I was in school, in the 1970's, I never heard the words – Affirmations, Visualization, Law of Attraction, Ho'oponopono, etc. *Yet, a few manifestations, unknowingly done, come to mind.*

1. In 1971, I won medals in the Karnataka State Athletics Association meet in Bangalore where I studied. All the

boys were older, taller and stronger. We won silver medals in volleyball and 4X100 metres relay and I was walking off when I heard my name being called. I won the bronze medal in Long Jump!!
2. In 1979, studying final year Engineering, the University Rank eluded me. I was obsessed about it and must have unknowingly manifested this. In the Final Semester, I got the sixth rank in Electrical Engineering, at Bangalore University!
3. In 1993, if my one-year-old daughter was in the car, I would get parking anywhere in Bangalore. It always happened, but on the flip side, if she wasn't there, I wouldn't get parking!

Then, as I learnt the power of Affirmations, Visualization, reading the book – "The Secret by Rhonda Byrne" and watching the 90-minute movie was a game changer. This really increased my self-belief, and I started practicing manifestation techniques seriously.

*After that several manifestations happened – Quit Smoking, Became Debt-Free, Bought my first Home, Changed profession successfully – from a Corporate Executive to Facilitator, Mentor & Coach, did MBA at age 53, learnt swimming at 49, reduced 11 kgs of bodyweight at 61 years, my two kids settling in Toronto, got 3 clients LMI World client of the year award, myself the LMI World Facilitator of the Year award thrice in a row, and many more.*

I quote my mentor - "**Affirmation is the befriending of the subconscious mind with the conscious mind to achieve my dreams, desires and goals.**"

It works on the theory of displacement – Positive thoughts replace the negative ones in our subconscious mind. Our manifestations happen as we think of what we want and the Law of Attraction kicks in.

Principles of Affirmations:

✓ ***Personal Pronoun – I, Me, My, Myself***
✓ ***Positively Stated***
✓ ***Present Continuous Tense***

Affirmation can be only for myself, not for others. But you must write your own Affirmations – Be specific.

What do I do next? Read them 10 times as soon as you wake up, 10 times just before sleeping at night and as many times as possible in between. Why early morning and night? That's when your conscious mind is drowsy, and your subconscious mind is wide awake (24 X 7). Why? The conscious mind is critical, discriminatory, logical, etc. So, it will be sceptical of the affirmations you repeat. That also is taken into the subconscious mind, since it is like a sponge and absorbs everything, it is told. Don't repeat them in front of sceptical people either.

What then is Visualization? It is a bright picture of the future. A pictorial form of My Affirmations is My Vision

Board. Add as many pictures as possible. Make a collage. Display it on your office desk and bedroom or have it as a screen saver in all gadgets.

Today, as a Life Coach & Mentor, I have helped many people to make their dreams come true – through Manifestation.

The practice of this doesn't involve magic but makes you act in ways that you ultimately get your manifestation. It attracts people and circumstances, opens doors and opportunities for the ultimate dream to manifest.

**My ultimate dream manifestation began around 10 months ago. On February 1$^{st}$, 2024, just 6 weeks after I had two stents placed in my heart, I enrolled in a Rs. 99/- 3-day course, which promised to make wannabe writers into successful authors.** It was from 7 pm to 9 pm on Thursday, Friday, and from 6 pm to 9 pm on Saturday. I enrolled in the program with absolutely no expectations, looking at the price tag. But I am a guy who gives everything to whatever I get into! **Also, from my teenage years, I have always wanted to write, because I was and still am a voracious reader!**

The Trainer / Coach, popularly known as "**Inspiring Jatin**", was making us engrossed in the science and art of becoming a successful author, with practical tools and the right examples, always action-oriented. On the second day, he "**left a tiger behind us**", which made us act. We announced to the world that midnight the name of the eBook and when it was being displayed on Amazon. **On 14th February, my first eBook – "How to change Habits – 10 secrets to Happiness", was on Amazon KDP. It became an Amazon #1 bestseller as promised by Jatin.** Just 11 days after I signed into the Program.

To participate in the first World Record as a team from "**International Council of Authors by Inspiring Jatin**", I wrote my second eBook by 28/02/2024. It also was an Amazon #1 bestseller, and **we got the World Record as well**.

Then **my third and 4th eBooks on Sales & Customer Retention happened one after another. These books were also Amazon #1 best-sellers.**

The first book was published as a printed version and the second one is getting ready to adorn the shelves of the World Delhi Book Fair. My first eBook was translated into Tamil and is now available on Amazon!

Last week, the team from ICA bagged another world record, where I was a participant. I am on course to be a part of an Anthology if I make it. ***If you are reading this piece in Anthology, I have once again manifested my dream.***

My sincere thanks to Inspiring Jatin and our 1300 strong networks for making this manifestation happen.

## About the Author

I am 67 years young, with exposure to several multinational brands, a Facilitator for Leadership Programs, a Life Coach and a Mentor to family-run businesses, often spanning two generations & to corporates too. I stay in Chennai & Erode and can be reached at 8807050018 or at suryaprakash2107@gmail.com.

# THE DANCE OF MANIFESTATION

### REDISCOVERING HAPPINESS THROUGH NATURE, LOSS, AND LETTING GO

### BY SHREE SHAMBAV

*D*uring my formative years, nature was my silent companion and sanctuary. The woods, timeless and enchanting, revealed surprises at every turn. Flowers whispered stories of resilience, blooming defiantly among thorns, while butterflies embodied transformation, teaching me the elegance of simplicity. Chasing dragonflies and kites filled my heart with unbridled joy, and the touch-me-nots, retreating at a touch, reflected the tender vulnerability of my soul.

Though scorpions and reptiles invoked fear, I embraced the rain like a child reunited with a loving mother, croaking like frogs, and cooing like cuckoos, oblivious to mud-streaked clothes or adult disapproval. Feeding sparrows and crows deepened my sense of connection to a delicate, harmonious ecosystem.

Sunlit days warmed my spirit, while starry nights whispered of infinity. The moon, a steadfast confidant, offered its radiant solace. In those pure, unfiltered moments, I discovered life's rhythm and the effortless joy born of a heart free from expectations.

## The Shift: From Harmony to Hustle

As I grew older, the innocence of childhood faded, replaced by the relentless pace of modern life. The artificial cadence of deadlines and meetings overtook the natural rhythm of seasons. Life became a whirlwind of achievements and metrics, chasing an elusive finish line without knowing why.

Then came the moment that altered everything: an unexpected loss that shattered the very foundation of my existence. It was as if the universe had pressed the pause button on my life. Grief consumed me, and in its wake, it left profound questions: Who am I? What am I running toward? And most importantly, why am I not happy?

One night, in the solitude of my despair, I sent a question into the cosmos: Why can't I be happy, even under pressure? Why can't I feel the joy I once knew as a child? It wasn't a structured prayer or a deliberate manifestation—it was a raw cry from the depths of my being.

## The Stranger's Smile: A Catalyst for Change

A few weeks later, I met someone who would unknowingly become a catalyst for my transformation. He was a simple man, radiating an infectious cheerfulness. His smile was so genuine it seemed to carry the world's weight lightly. Intrigued, I asked, "How can you be so happy, even with life's challenges?"

He looked at me, his eyes sparkling with wisdom, and replied, "We have one journey. Why not make it a happy one?"

His words struck a chord deep within me. That night, I couldn't stop thinking: Why am I chasing validation from others? Why does it matter if I'm not the smartest, richest, or most powerful? If I'm not rich within myself, what's the point of external wealth?

## Letting Go of the Baggage

This revelation caused a significant internal upheaval. I realised that happiness wasn't something I could acquire externally—it had to be cultivated within. The first bold step I took was to leave the corporate world. I walked away from the hefty pay checks, the prestigious title, and the societal validation. It wasn't easy; every fibre of my being resisted the change.

I started a small organisation where I could operate on my terms and under less pressure. I moved closer to nature, building a small estate where I could reconnect with the simplicity I had once known. However, this journey was not as simple as I had anticipated. It was agonising to let go of everything I believed mattered most—my position, network, and comfort. Each step of shedding this "baggage" felt like losing a part of myself.

At times, I felt betrayed by the universe. I had manifested happiness, but instead, I was encountering pain and challenges. It was as if the universe was testing my resolve, pushing me to transform on every level—physically, emotionally, and mentally.

## The Morphism of Manifestation

Slowly, I began to understand the purpose behind these struggles. Manifestation isn't a magic wand; it's a process of becoming. It's like a seed planted in the soil—it doesn't bloom instantly. First, it must break apart in the darkness, its outer shell cracking open to allow growth. This is the morphism of manifestation, the painful yet necessary process of shedding old identities to make way for the new.

The universe wasn't handing me happiness on a silver platter; it was guiding me toward it by stripping away everything that wasn't essential. As I embraced minimalism—both in material possessions and in my mental clutter—I began to see life with greater clarity. The cosmos started to reveal its beauty and rhythm once again, just as it had in my childhood.

## Manifestation and the Power of Intent

This journey taught me that manifestation is far more profound than simply wishing for something. It requires clarity of intent, the courage to face discomfort, and the willingness to let go of what no longer serves us. When we declare our desires to the universe, we are also committing to the growth required to align with those desires.

The process is rarely linear. It's chaotic, challenging, and, at times, disheartening. But if we trust the divine flow and stay true to our intentions, the universe responds in ways we can't always foresee. It orchestrates opportunities, removes barriers, and guides us toward our highest potential.

Today, as I look around at the life I've created—a life filled with nature, purpose, and joy—I feel an overwhelming sense of gratitude. The journey back to happiness wasn't easy, but it was worth every step. The whispers of the cosmos are always there, waiting for us to listen, trust, and take that leap of faith.

## About the Author

Shree Shambav is a best-selling author, inspirational speaker, philanthropist, life coach, and entrepreneur. Celebrated for his transformative insights, he has touched countless lives through his profound writings, impactful lectures, and compassionate guidance. With a rare ability to inspire deep personal growth and meaningful transformation, Shree Shambav continues to empower individuals to unlock their fullest potential and embrace purposeful living.

Shree Shambav founded the Ayur Rakshita Foundation, which promotes limitless expansion, universal brotherhood, and environmental preservation. The nonprofit assists many communities while striving for societal change.

To learn more about Shree Shambav and his works, go to www.shambav.org.

# MANIFESTING THE UNSEEN

## A JOURNEY OF FAITH AND INTENTION

## BY NITA RATHOD

*A* few years ago, I participated in a program encouraging us to envision and create our future. Towards the end of the program, we were asked to write down our deepest desires—our dreams for five years ahead. I was hesitant, almost resistant. How could simply writing something on paper possibly shape someone's future? The idea seemed absurd, even laughable. I felt unprepared and unconvinced. But with the gentle insistence of the facilitators, I wrote down five wishes spanning different areas of my life. One of them scribbled with indifference, was: *"My son will get admission to IIT."*

I did not think much of it. I folded the paper, put it in a cupboard, and entirely forgot about it. Back then, I had no concept of manifestation. I had no idea what the word really meant. Life carried on, and the forgotten paper sat accumulating dust over the years. One day, when cleaning out the cupboard, I came across the hidden page. I was astonished as I unfolded it and read the lines. Every wish I had written had been granted. Among them was the seemingly unachievable dream of my son getting a spot at IIT. I stood there in disbelief. How is this possible? At first, I discounted it as a coincidence.

But then, I came across the movie *The Secret,* and it was like holding a mirror to my own experience. The film made me revisit that moment when I had written down my dreams. Slowly, I began to connect the dots. I realised that by writing down those wishes; I had unknowingly sent them out into the cosmos. And the universe, in its mysterious way, had responded.

When I glanced back, I noticed how possibilities had coincided flawlessly, almost as if guided by an unseen power. Some roads were uncertain and difficult, but I had no choice but to act. Despite the discomfort and uncertainty, each step—whether deliberate or instinctive—brought us closer to the dream I had penned on that forgotten paper. It felt as if the cosmos was orchestrating events for my benefit. That's when I started to believe in the power of something bigger—faith in the divine, confidence in the universe, or perhaps just faith in the sheer strength of intention.

When my son cleared his JEE Mains and Advanced, I was overjoyed and proud. But our journey wasn't over yet. The next step—filling out the choice list for IIT admissions—brought its wave of anxiety. My husband and I, both from medical backgrounds, were completely unfamiliar with the process. We feared making a mistake that could jeopardise his chances. We felt lost and overwhelmed.

Just when our doubt reached its peak, something extraordinary happened. A neighbour who had moved away years ago unexpectedly called me. She mentioned that her son was coming to Ahmedabad for his UPSC exam and asked if I could assist them during their visit. At the time, I had no idea that her son had graduated from IIT Bombay. When they arrived, I casually shared my confusion and concerns about the choice-filling process. Without hesitation, she offered her son's help.

Her son came to our home and patiently explained the importance of making informed decisions during the choice-filling process. His insights and guidance cleared our doubts and gave us the confidence we desperately needed. It was as if the universe had placed him in our path at just the right moment. With his help, my son filled out his choices with clarity and conviction. Soon after, he received admission to IIT—a dream I had unknowingly manifested years ago as part of an exercise I didn't even believe in.

This experience transformed me. It taught me a profound lesson: when we declare our intentions with clarity and faith, the universe begins to align in ways we cannot comprehend. The journey wasn't easy, and it wasn't without its share of struggles and uncertainties, but each step—no matter how difficult—led us closer to a dream that once seemed impossible.

Today, I wholeheartedly believe in the power of manifestation, the strength of intention, and the magic of trusting the unknown. Sometimes, the answers we seek are already on their way, waiting for us to take a leap of faith. The universe is always listening—it's up to us to trust its timing and guidance.

## About the Author

Dr. Nita Rathod, an associate professor in the Physiology Department at Narendra Modi Medical College, Ahmedabad, is a passionate seeker of wisdom and a storyteller of the human spirit. Encounters with people from all walks of life have enriched her journey, each story inspiring her to reflect on one of life's greatest mysteries: What is love?

Through years of introspection, Dr. Rathod realised that love is more than an emotion—it's a guiding force that shapes our choices, fuels our dreams, and gives meaning to our lives. Her book, Unlocking 10 Secrets of Love, is the culmination of this profound quest to understand love in all its beauty, contradictions, and power.

The inspiration for this journey came from a simple yet powerful horoscope that read, "The impossible journey is the one that never begins. Your time is limited, so don't waste it living someone else's life." These words ignited a fire within her, pushing her to explore love's many dimensions.

Her work is more than a book—it's an invitation to discover love's transformative power, not just in relationships, but in the way we see ourselves. Dr. Rathod's insights offer readers a chance to unlock love's true essence and embrace its ability to heal, connect, and inspire.

# HOPELESSNESS TO HOPEFULNESS: MY MOTHERHOOD MANIFESTATION JOURNEY

## BY MANEESHA SINGH

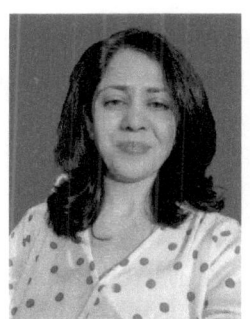

$\mathcal{T}$he hospital room was glowing with white lights, but it felt like a storm raged within. I lay there, exhausted and restless after 16 hours of intense labour pain. Every contraction had been a trial, each one bringing me closer to meeting the little life I had nurtured within me for nine months. We were very excited. The whole family was praying for our baby's safe arrival.

I and my husband always wanted to have a girl child. We had already decided her name. Before getting admitted to the hospital, we had done all the decorations and made all arrangements to welcome her home.

Then, the unthinkable happened. The doctor entered the room; her expression was calm but serious. "We have been monitoring the baby's heart rate, "It is dropping. It is an emergency. We cannot promise anything but we will try our best. We need emergency C-section immediately." Her tone was full of urgency.

I froze. My heart skipped a beat as the words sank in. We were expecting a smooth, normal delivery. I felt my body was betraying me. My world spun and a wave of panic ran through every cell of my body.

I glanced at my husband, who looked pale and shaken, and then at my mother, whose hands were clasped tightly in prayer. I saw my fear mirrored in their eyes. And in that instant, I realized the need to let go of my fear and trust in our highest good.

I closed my eyes and took a deep breath. Memories of a meditation class came up in my mind. It was about the power of affirmations. Good positive words and sentences could help manifest any desired results. It felt like something; I could hold onto in that gloomy moment.

"Everything is good. My baby is safe. She is good. We both are strong," I whispered to myself.

I chanted this affirmation like a mantra. With every repetition, I visualized my thoughts and emotions. I imagined my baby safe and healthy. I imagined my baby's heartbeat growing strong. I visualized myself holding my baby; I felt tiny fingers touching my cheek.

My family too joined my hand. My husband and my mother started praying with faith in their hearts. Slowly, our whole clan joined in from their respective places. We all had hope and faith in our hearts and minds. We all had created a bubble of positive and protective energy with love and faith.

The medical team was busy preparing for the C-section. I kept chanting my affirmations in my head. I was wheeled into the operating theatre. I kept chanting and never left faith. My body was tired but my belief was solid that everything is good.

The lights in the operating theatre were very bright and the beeping sounds of machines were constantly reminding the seriousness of the moment. Amidst it all, I kept repeating my affirmations. Each word felt like a navigator, helping me to reach and connect with the life inside my womb.

The medical team worked with precision and calmness. I heard the continuous sound of machines and short instructions exchanged between the doctors and nurses. And then, amidst the cold and fear, came the moment I had been waiting for.

The sound I had been waiting for, the very first cry of my daughter. A sharp cry pierced the air, shattering the tension. It was the most beautiful sound I had ever heard. My happiness soared, and tears rolled down my face as the doctor announced, "It's a girl. She is healthy and fine." My heart echoed, "My love is safe, she is here".

The first glimpse of her tiny face took my breath away. Her eyes, wide and curious, locked onto mine as though she knew exactly who I was. That gaze was not just a look, it was a connection, a silent understanding that we were meant to be together.

The doctor brought her close to me, her cheek brushing against mine, soft and warm like a whisper of love. Her touch sent a wave of warmth through my entire body. I felt joy and gratitude. I held my child, my daughter in my arms. Her beautiful face took away all my exhaustion, pain, and fear.

When I look back, I realize that the affirmations made a difference; they changed everything for my good. They gave me strength in my weak moments and hope in despair. They keep reminding me that even in the gloomy days, there is power in faith, love, and the words we speak.

I promised myself and my daughter that I would teach her the power of faith and hope. I promised to remind her that even in the most uncertain situations; we should have faith in the universe for our highest good.

Life will not work as per plan always. But that does not mean that we feel hopeless. How we respond to uncertainties is absolutely in our hands. We should affirm for good and believe in miracles, even in the darkest days.

This story of my child's birth is a testament to the power of affirmation and the strength of our soul. It is a perfect reminder that we can manifest everything with hope and faith. A miracle happens in life with the honest and continuous practice of affirmations.

So, everyone reading my manifestation story let me tell you that you, too, have that power. Believe me that power is within you. Trust the power within you. It will guide you in the difficult times. Belief in your heart is very powerful in manifesting what your heart truly longs for.

## About the Author

Maneesha Singh is an entrepreneur, author and a mother. She is a firm believer in the power of faith and the universe. She has experienced the power of manifestation and inspires others to believe in their inner potential. In this Anthology, she shares her motherhood manifestation journey to inspire you to believe in the power of faith, love, and the words you speak.

# MIRACLES UNFOLD: MANIFESTING LAND, HOME, AND BESTSELLER STATUS

## BY DR. DEEPA DIDDDI

*T*hings often happen when one least expects them! Opportunity often takes one by surprise unless one is prepared for it. As an academician, I have always advocated being prepared for any eventuality. However, we often forget our own advice. I will share my own story today about how I forgot to follow what I preached until one day, I picked up the threads and started following diligently.

My journey of Manifestation began after I came out of my class one day in 2022 when I motivated my students to maintain a journal. Research says that those who write down their goals are more likely to succeed. I realized that I had let go of this habit for years. I reached home, took out a diary, and started writing about my day-to-day activities. Slowly, I began to put my desires onto paper, and one day, I wrote three major goals I wanted to achieve in the next two years:

A decent home, Becoming an Author, and Working in the Energy Realm

I wrote down my desires without any idea of how and when I would be able to fulfil them. I just followed what I told my students during my lectures: dream big, fuel your desires by taking small but planned and strategized steps, and the gold is yours! That is what I did.

I started by making a pictorial grid, writing positive questions, and repeating them to myself daily.

## The Power of Manifestation Techniques

### Pictorial Grid

I used three major techniques to manifest the above three things for myself. I created a pictorial grid with the image of my dream house, a picture of book content being created, images of a woman with golden light, stars, and planets, and a few more generalized images to enhance and support these three major goals.

I made this grid the wallpaper of my phone screen, took a laminated printout, and kept it on my study table. The purpose was simple: I would look at it throughout the day and send repeated signals to my subconscious to achieve them.

## Positive Affirmative Questions

I would repeat the following affirmations throughout the day, with a focus in the morning before I got out of bed and at night just before I went to sleep. I would also spend time looking at my grid while affirming the statements.

"Why do I always get help from unexpected people and situations that help me grow and achieve my targets?"

"What land is the Universe sending my way to build my dream home?"

"Why is it that Universe gives me novel ideas on how to write my book?"

"What bestselling book am I writing?"

Within a fortnight of practicing the affirmations, I stumbled upon an article on Akashic Reading. I was intrigued. I was practicing Yoga, so I was aware of the elements and the importance of the realm of Akasha. I dug deeper and called a friend to discuss Akashic Reading with her. She told me she would do a gift reading for me as an Akashic Reader. I was surprised since I was not aware that she was one! After the gift reading I took the contact details of the Akashic Trainer from her I joined the workshop in December and became an advanced-level Akashic reader. That was the beginning of my journey of magic and manifestations. I did all the course levels and spent considerable time with the Akasha Tatva.

I continued with the two techniques mentioned above, the pictorial grid and the affirmative questions, and I included visualization and gratitude as a daily practice. I started picturing the house as I wanted, and before going to bed, I would express my immense gratitude to the universe for manifesting my desire to experience the element of Akasha in this physical dimension.

My husband's impending superannuation in 2023 made me restless to look for a comfortable, decent living space. I continued the practice, and despite initial financial constraints, we secured a plot in the exact surroundings I had visualized. More surprising was that the architects we hired put the design I had thought of during my meditative practice on paper. The elevation matched the grid picture in totality. I was amazed at the precision of Manifestation. I had read about these things and heard about them, but I was now experiencing and living them. "The best was yet to be!"

I attended the workshop by *Inspiring Jatin* in October 2024 to manifest my long dream of becoming an author. As a person of habit, I spend about two hours on social media weekly and on specified days. Surprisingly, just after getting up one morning, I picked up the phone, looked at the grid, did my affirmations, and opened my Facebook account. I came across *Inspiring Jatin's* advertisement and joined the workshop. My friends and I had been talking and planning to write a book for over three to four years. I had been passionate about writing a book, focusing on management studies for academic purposes. I had penned down initial pages, aiming to publish in 2025. Every time I would sit down to write, I would be dissatisfied and start all over again.

That unexpected advertisement on Facebook that caught my attention: "Inspiring Jatin's transformative workshop," changed my direction and inspired me to pursue a realistic and engaging subject that would help people connect to themselves and others meaningfully.

In just a few weeks, my book took shape. The words flowed effortlessly as if inspired by an invisible force. I wrote with clarity, passion, and purpose. The manuscript grew, and so did my excitement. I published "Staying Connected:

7 Effective Strategies to Unleash Your Authentic Self" on November 26, 2024, within a month of the workshop.

This is the power of Manifestation!

## Simultaneous Manifestations

As I focused on my desires by taking action, remarkable things unfolded. Our dream home has neared completion, reflecting our vision of comfort and sustainability. My book, published on November 26, 2024, shot to the top of Amazon's bestseller list in two categories! I was overwhelmed with joy, knowing my message resonated with others. I am an Akashic Reader and a Trainer.

## Conclusion

Looking back, I realize Manifestation is about alignment, trust, and gratitude. My manifestation journey teaches that anything is possible when we align our energy, thoughts, and emotions in the right direction and act when opportunity knocks. I encourage you to explore your deepest desires. Remember, miracles unfold when we trust ourselves and the universe.

# MY MANIFESTATION JOURNEY: FROM SELF DOUBT, SELF HATE, AND IGNORANT STUDENT TO A CONFIDENT, LOVABLE, FAMILIAR DOCTOR

## BY DR SATHYA PRIYANKA

## Introduction

How would it feel for a young girl under 11 to experience puberty far earlier than expected, unable to understand the changes happening to her body and mind? How did she navigate each day, grappling with confusion and unanswered questions? Can you imagine her thoughts and struggles? Did she ever find the answers her mind was desperately seeking?

This is the transformation journey of a girl who, despite being unprepared to handle her body and mind during her early years, grew into a renowned doctor specializing in physical, psychological, and gender/sexual health for children, teens, and adults. Are you curious to discover what shaped her remarkable transformation? If so, let's begin her story now.

## Journey of a Self-doubt, Self-hate, Ignorant Girl

In sixth grade, I went through puberty, which brought with it, significant physical changes: weight gain, hair growth, spots, and excessive sweating. These changes were incredibly painful, and I regretted my pre-pubescent appearance and my carefree childhood. Puberty brought limitations, including not being able to dress the way I wanted. As a child, I loved wearing T-shirts and shorts like a boy and imitating male heroes, imagining myself as such. However, puberty brought breast growth, fat accumulation, and body changes that shattered my self-image. I had a hard time dealing with my appearance, often crying alone, and wondering why these changes were happening. I even faced ridicule from my classmates about my appearance, which made me even more self-conscious.

Although my family provided a safe and supportive environment, I was hesitant to share my feelings. I was overwhelmed with countless questions:

What is puberty? Why me? How do I cope with these changes? One day, during an open conversation with my grandmother and aunt about relationships and boundaries, I mustered up the courage to ask them about the changes in my body. They assured me that these changes were natural for all girls. Although their answers made sense, I felt isolated, questioning my gender identity due to my preference to be recognized as a boy.

Feeling misunderstood, I decided to suppress my questions and feelings. My family and friends tried to comfort me with explanations, but their rational answers did not address my deeper issues. This silence marked a period of confusion and self-discovery in my adolescence.

## My Manifestation journey

I had a habit of reading weekly magazines, and one day, I came across the quote, "What we think, we become" by Buddha. This simple statement transformed my perspective, making me realize that my thoughts, not fate, shaped my life. I began changing my beliefs about my body and appearance, learning how thoughts manifest into reality. Over two years of inner battles, I developed a positive self-image and decided to take control of my body and mind. I visualized myself as a doctor and counsellor, especially for children, aiming to help them overcome challenges similar to mine.

Every night before sleeping, I visualized my future as a doctor and an angelic friend who would support me throughout life. This practice inspired me to study harder and build self-love through positive affirmations and forgiveness. In 11th grade, new students joined our school, and one became my close friend. Surprisingly, she embodied the angel I had visualized. Her love and care confirmed this, even though she was in a different section.

In 12th grade, during a severe cold, I attended school despite my discomfort. The next day, my friend brought me medicine and astonished me with her thoughtfulness. She bought it from her father after school. Her care strengthened our bond, and we began studying together for the board exams. She even called me daily over the phone to wake me up for study sessions.

With my efforts, family support, and friend's encouragement, I scored the marks required to pursue my dream. I got into medical college and fulfilled my goal of becoming a doctor, ready to help others as I had always envisioned.

## Conclusion

My journey has taught me that we manifest what we believe and think about ourselves. I transformed from a self-doubting, self-hating, and ignorant student into a confident, loving, and well-known doctor through visualization, positive affirmations, and self-talk. I manifested my profession by completing both my undergraduate and postgraduate studies at the same college.

Today, I run my clinic dedicated to helping adolescents and adults struggling with poor self-image, low self-esteem, and gender-related confusion during adolescence. Although I was an introvert in my school days, my manifestation practices have enabled me to become a keynote speaker. I now create awareness among students in schools and ashrams, emphasizing the importance of knowledge about physical, psychological, and gender/sexual health.

## About the Author

I am Dr. Sathya Priyanka, a doctor, counsellor, bestselling author of the e-book "Top Secrets to Make Your Child a Big Asset of the World – Series on Amazon", and a speaker. I am on a mission to impact one million children, teens, and adults by raising awareness about identity, personality, gender, and sexuality, helping them become extraordinary individuals on this planet.

So far, I have helped hundreds of students discover their purpose and unlock their potential. I believe that sharing my manifestation story will add immense value to readers and inspire them to achieve their goals in life.

Regards,

Dr Sathya Priyanka, Siddha Physician & counsellor for children Teens Adults

- Parents Teens Mentor
- Registration No 5239
- Founder of: Body Soul Mind Care Siddha Clinic, Ilanji, Tamil Nadu, India
- Offering below services:
  - Consultation
  - Counselling
  - Varmam
  - Mentorship for Personal development
  - Mental health education
  - Sexual health education for Children, Teens, Adults, Queer

- For doubts, feedback, appointment: https://linktr.ee/drsathyapriyanka
- Follow me @DrSathyaPriyanka

# THE POWER OF MANIFESTATION: A JOURNEY TO DREAM FULFILMENT

## BY THANDAVARAYAN M.

## Introduction

Rayan's story is a testament to the transformative power of manifestation. A dedicated professional in the supply chain management field, he had always dreamed of advancing his career to new heights. However, like many of us, he found himself constrained by self-doubt and limiting beliefs about what he could achieve.

## The Desire and the Journey

One day, while browsing online, Rayan stumbled upon videos about the Law of Attraction and manifestation. Intrigued, he began to immerse himself in this new world of possibilities. He participated in meditation programs, gratitude practices, and visualization exercises, slowly but surely rewiring his mindset from one of scarcity to abundance.

Rayan set a clear goal for himself: to become a Manager at a reputable company. He began to live "as if" he had already achieved this position, visualizing himself in the role every day. He updated his resume, reached out to contacts on LinkedIn, and most importantly, worked on removing his internal negative emotions and beliefs through daily meditation and visualization.

As he continued his manifestation journey, Rayan remembered a piece of advice he had heard: to treat job interviews as a "cakewalk." He began thanking potential interviewers in advance for the opportunity, visualizing himself in the office, surrounded by satisfied colleagues.

Then, on an ordinary Saturday, something extraordinary happened. Rayan received a call from an HR representative at Infosys, a major multinational corporation in India. This wasn't just any job opportunity – it was for the position of Head for the Infosys, a role even more senior than the one he had been manifesting.

The interview process was unlike anything Rayan had experienced before. There were no formal interviews, just two brief discussions. The first call, on Monday, was with the Corporate GM from Bangalore, who simply asked when he could join if offered the position. The second call, equally brief, was with the vice president from Bangalore.

Rayan was amazed. Everything was unfolding exactly as he had visualized, but even better than he had imagined. The final call came on Wednesday – it was HR, ready to discuss him package. To his amazement, they offered him a 50% increase from his previous salary.

On 3rd Dec 2015, Rayan stepped into his new role as Sr. Process Lead at Infosys, heading the Procurement role at Infosys. He had manifested not just a job, but a position that exceeded his original goal, showcasing the incredible potential of manifestation when combined with action and belief.

## Rayan's story illustrates the core principles of manifestation:

1. **Clear Intention:** He set a specific goal for his career advancement.
2. **Belief:** Through consistent visualization and positive affirmations, he cultivated a strong belief in his ability to achieve his goal.

3. **Aligned Action:** He updated his resume and networked on LinkedIn, taking tangible steps towards his goal.
4. **Letting Go:** By treating interviews as a "cakewalk," he released anxiety and attachment to outcomes.
5. **Gratitude:** He practiced daily gratitude, both for what he had and for the opportunity he believed was coming.

Manifestation isn't just about positive thinking; it's about aligning our thoughts, emotions, and actions with our desires. It's about opening ourselves up to possibilities beyond what we initially imagined, as Rayan discovered when he manifested an even better position than he had initially sought.

As Rayan's experience shows, manifestation can be a powerful tool for personal and professional growth. It encourages us to dream big, believe in ourselves, and take inspired action towards our goals. While results may not always be as dramatic or swift as in this case, the practice of manifestation can lead us to opportunities and achievements we might never have thought possible.

Remember, manifestation is not about controlling every aspect of our lives, but about aligning ourselves with our deepest desires and remaining open to the surprising and wonderful ways the universe might bring them to fruition. Rayan's story serves as an inspiring reminder of the potential we all hold within us to manifest our dreams into reality.

## About the Author

**Thandavarayan M.**

Self-motivated, dependable and dedicated professional, has 24+ years of experience in the field of procurement and supply chain management. Working as a Manager, Master Data Management, Vendor master maintenance & digitalization of procurement for India's leading health care provider.

## Education:

- Pursuing "Executive Program in Data Science & Digital Transformation", from IIT Guwahati.
- "Global Certificate in Data Science and AI", from Accredian.
- Post Graduate Diploma in Materials Management, Indian School of Business Management
- MBA in Sikkim Manipal University.
- BSc (Psychology) in the University of Madras.
- D.S.C.M.T (Diploma in Self-Confidence and Motivation Training) in Human Resource Development and research organization.
- PGDCA (Post Graduate Diploma in Computer Application) in the Tamil Nadu Computer Development System.

> D. Pharmacy in Padmavathi College of Pharmacy, Dharmapuri, TN

## Contact

WhatsApp Group: https://chat.whatsapp.com/FfZd0cqRFvLI7bCjJXkGgl

Telegram: Telegram: Contact @gsw291

Gmail: gsw2912023@gmail.com

LinkedIn: https://www.linkedin.com/in/mtrayan

YouTube: https://www.youtube.com/@GSW291/featured

Facebook: https://www.facebook.com/profile.php?id=61550375726343

Instagram: https://www.instagram.com/mtrayan34/

Podcast: https://podcasters.spotify.com/pod/show/mtrayan

https://open.spotify.com/show/6kzieUsCR9qcth0owDSTGk

## Acknowledgments

My heartfelt gratitude to Mr. **Inspiring Jatin** for his exceptional guidance and encouragement in my journey through self-publishing book coaching. Mr. Jatin's insightful mentorship has been a beacon of inspiration, enlightening the complex path of bringing a book to completion. His expertise, coupled with a genuine passion for empowering aspiring authors, has been instrumental in honing my writing skills and navigating the complexities of the publishing process. Under Jatin's guidance, I have not only discovered the shades of storytelling but also gained confidence in my ability to share my narrative with the world. I am immensely thankful for Inspiring Jatin's firm support and transformative coaching.

# HEALING THROUGH MANIFESTATION: MY JOURNEY TO WELLNESS AND EMPOWERMENT

## BY DR. PRATIBHAA BORADE

### Introduction

Six years ago, my life took a turn that left me feeling helpless and defeated. As a paediatrician, mother of two, and fitness enthusiast, I prided myself on maintaining an active and balanced lifestyle. But when I developed a debilitating frozen shoulder, my world shrank. The pain was excruciating, and the restricted mobility made even the simplest tasks impossible. I could no longer exercise, drive, or enjoy my profession. For someone who had always embraced challenges with resilience, this period tested my mental and physical strength in ways I had never experienced. Little did I know that this struggle would lead me to a life-changing journey of manifestation and self-transformation.

## The Desire and the Journey

My frozen shoulder started as a minor inconvenience—a dull ache and slight stiffness in my right shoulder. Over time, the pain became unbearable, and I couldn't move my arm at all. Nights were sleepless, days were filled with frustration, and my once-active life seemed like a distant memory. The inability to function as a doctor and mother weighed heavily on me. My diabetes worsened, and I gained weight, further compounding my distress.

Though I'd faced many challenges before—from balancing a demanding career with raising two daughters to overcoming personal setbacks—this time was different. I felt hopeless. Traditional treatments, including medications and physiotherapy, provided no relief. For the first time in my life, I thought I'd have to accept a diminished quality of life. My only desire was simple yet profound: to heal my shoulder, regain control of my diabetes, and return to my vibrant, active self.

During this dark phase, I stumbled upon the concept of manifestation and the Law of Attraction. I had read about it earlier, but this time, it resonated deeply. I decided to embrace it fully. If I could not find relief through conventional means, perhaps the power of the mind could help me heal.

## The Manifestation Process

With renewed hope, I immersed myself in the practices of manifestation. I bought notebooks for scripting, dedicated time for meditation, and started journaling my gratitude daily. I wrote affirmations as if my dreams had already come true: "I am cured of my shoulder pain. My diabetes is under control. I am living a healthy, active life." Visualization became a daily ritual—I pictured myself lifting weights at the gym, driving without discomfort, and enjoying life to its fullest.

One significant step was joining a program focused on freedom from diabetes. This program introduced advanced manifestation techniques and reinforced my belief in the power of the mind. Alongside these practices, I followed my doctor's advice and took an injection to relieve the pain. This combination of medical treatment and manifestation created a powerful synergy. Slowly but surely, I started noticing changes.

The shift wasn't just physical; it was mental and emotional too. I felt lighter, more optimistic, and deeply connected to my goals. The pain began to subside, and my shoulder's mobility improved. Within weeks, I could perform movements that had seemed impossible for years. My doctors were amazed by the rapid progress.

I returned to the gym and gradually resumed weight training. Each day, I felt stronger and more confident. My diabetes improved significantly, and I reduced my medication from five tablets to just one. These results reaffirmed my faith in manifestation and motivated me to continue. I created a vision board filled with images and affirmations representing my ideal life. Each day, I spent time with my board, visualizing and feeling gratitude for the life I was creating.

## Conclusion and Lessons Learned

This journey taught me the profound impact of aligning thoughts, emotions, and actions with our desires. Manifestation isn't about wishing for miracles; it's about transforming our mindset, embracing gratitude, and taking inspired action. The power to heal and achieve lies within each of us.

Today, I am healthier, stronger, and more at peace than ever before. I've learned to forgive, let go of past grievances, and approach life with renewed positivity. Manifestation has not only healed my body but also reshaped my outlook. If I can achieve this transformation, so can you. Dream big, believe in the impossible, and take the first step toward manifesting your ideal life.

## About the Author

I am Dr. Pratibhaa Borade, a paediatrician, mother of two, and wellness enthusiast. Despite being a diabetic for eight years, I have always prioritized physical fitness and a balanced lifestyle. Through my journey with manifestation, I've overcome significant challenges, including a frozen shoulder, and rediscovered my passion for health and vitality. I hope my story inspires you to harness the power of manifestation and create a life of abundance and joy.

# MANIFESTING THE YOGIC WAY

## BY SUCHITA SANJAY

*A* few deep soul-calling moments in my late forties helped me see my innate ability to be empathetic, which inspired me to begin my career as a Hypnotherapist. These incidents lit up the fire in me to lead a more meaningful and purposeful life by empowering others to embrace Happy Minds and Abundant Lives. I am glad I took that plunge as today I have the deep satisfaction of transforming over 400 people globally leading happy and abundant lives.

As a student of Siddha Yoga, which means 'Yoga of Accomplishment'. My Guru Pashupathi taught us about Iccha, Kriya and Gnana. The Yogic method of manifestation entailed first having "Iccha" which means the desire and intention backed with a purpose that will bring happiness to others as well as me. "Kriya" means taking action to follow the purpose of aiming to solve other's problems. "Gnana" means acquiring the required knowledge and skills to solve one's problems. To achieve all of the above the grace of God which means "Anugraha" is also very important.

**Iccha – "The Desire"** – The desire to empower people with happy minds and abundant lives was extremely evident, but the difficulty was that I had no expertise in psychology as I came from a commerce background. Being in my late forties also raised the question of will I be able to cop and also find a course that would be suitable for me. Nothing materialised for six months, yet I didn't give up and continued looking. I recall meeting a woman and having an uncontrollable thought: "I hope this person is not suffering from cancer as I can see a lot of suppression in the face". That day, my thoughts were, "How could I even think like that?" But I also realized I had no control over it. Within three days, I learned that the woman was battling cancer. That night, I was crying and asking my masters to show me a path. As tears rolled down, I decided to check my phone again to see if I could find anything. I remember it was a click by chance, that I came across a course called Rapid Transformational Therapy, which was a hybrid therapeutic approach combining the best principles of neuroscience such as hypnotherapy, CBT, Psychotherapy, regression and other modalities of healing, and I decided that it was the one for me. This was when I realised when the calling is deep and you surrender to the universe it has its own way of leading you to manifest what you want.

**Kriya – "The Action"** – "Karmanye vadhikaraste ma phaleshu kadachana" which mean "You have the right to perform your duty/action, but not to the fruits thereof". Following this principle from the Bhagavad Gita has helped me to take Action combined with Consistency and Discipline leading to manifest the desired life. This sutra hooked me to take action in the direction of my goals and show up for myself and for others every single day. When we take consistent action with discipline and dedication life also makes sure we are in the right place at the right time. This taking action led me to learn and set myself up for the profession.

**Gnana – "The Knowledge"** – Learning hypnotherapy was a lot of fun, and I finished it successfully to become a licensed clinical hypnotherapist. The real test then arrived. I wasn't really tech-savvy or interested in social networking. My mind was filled with self-doubt, so I used what I had learned from hypnotherapy to fight it like a warrior right from understanding the root cause of the subconscious wiring I had given myself regarding self-doubt, to rewire my mind with powerful suggestions and strong visualisations of the desired life I want. I even learned from various coaches, from setting up a Zoom call with my clients because COVID was at its worst at the time. Since I was really against social media and I had to fight this resistance; I knew I had to change as the world was changing. Clearly having a social media presence was one of the ways to get the word out and draw in the right people to provide services. I recall one of my coaches asking me this profound question "Is your purpose greater than your limitations?" This question hit me like a ton of bricks, and I realized that if I want to help others and improve the world, I cannot hide. Ultimately, I needed to grasp the fundamentals of managing my social media accounts. I realised that learning should be constant. This year I was so happy to have learnt powerful yogic techniques to help my clients using a blend of approaches and the results are phenomenal.

**Anugraha – Who I am with the grace of God** – If you have read this all along here is just a little bit about me. As a Clinical Hypnotherapist and a mindset coach using yogic techniques, I have impacted over 400 lives spanning more than 8 countries in 1:1 sessions. I specialize in personalized sessions, aiding clients in overcoming anxiety, fears, depression, and mindset issues. Together, dispelling limiting beliefs, fostering self-esteem, confidence, and self-belief.

My influence reaches globally, touching lives across the USA, Canada, Australia, South Africa, Cape Verde, Indonesia, Dubai, Cameroon, England, and India. I have authored the book 'Miracle "Trance"formations' under the guidance of Inspiring Jatin. I was honoured to be a part of history with the International Council of Authors who together released 40 e-books in just 24 hours setting a World Record for the maximum number of E-books published in a day.

I am a recipient of the Outstanding Leadership Award conferred by Health 2.0 Conferences, Las Vegas 2024. Some of my articles are published in national and international newspapers and e-magazines. I have also been on podcasts with hosts on their channel and have conducted a few online classes on mindset issues in India and in collaboration with JP Health & Wellness, USA.

You can find me on https://suchitasanjay.com/

# MANIFESTING MIRACLES: HOW I MET THE PRESIDENT OF INDIA 2023

## BY MAINO MURMU

### Introduction

Eighteen years—it's a long time to be away from the people and places that shaped you. My journey to America had been filled with dreams and challenges but also brought sacrifices. I had left behind family, traditions, and a part of myself. When I finally visited India, it was an emotional homecoming. My mother, now in her mid-60s, had aged in ways that startled and moved me.

This visit wasn't just about reconnecting with family. It was also a journey of self-discovery. As I trained to become a health coach, I delved deeply into India's rich culture and traditions. Amidst this, an extraordinary event unfolded—a woman from my community became the President of India. Her achievement filled me with pride, and a strong desire took root in my heart: I wanted to meet her. This desire wasn't just about her status; it was about the inspiration her journey represented and the sense of connection I felt to her success.

## The Desire and the Journey

Meeting the President of India seemed like an unattainable dream. My friends and family gently reminded me of the barriers—her busy schedule, the protocols, and my own limited connections. With my return ticket to the U.S. already booked, time was slipping away. Yet, the desire to meet her grew stronger. It wasn't just admiration; it felt personal. I wanted to congratulate her and share the pride of our community's collective achievement.

Despite numerous attempts, there was no clear path to secure an appointment. Still, I refused to give up. During conversations with family, my mother, with optimism, said, "Don't worry, we'll meet her." Her faith gave me hope, and I decided to leave no stone unturned.

As the days passed, I felt both frustrated and determined. A surprising turn of events came through a distant relative, who informed me that there was a possibility of meeting the President on August 15th—India's Independence Day. This news brought both excitement and urgency. However, this new plan clashed with my scheduled flight to the U.S., adding another layer of complication.

Understanding the moment's importance, my brother stepped in and rearranged my plans. He cancelled my original ticket and booked a new one despite the financial strain it caused. His support bolstered my resolve. As the appointment day approached, I felt an overwhelming mix of anticipation and gratitude.

## The Manifestation Process

The desire to meet the President had consumed my thoughts. With no guarantee of success, I turned to manifestation. Every night, I wrote my wish on a piece of paper: "I will meet the President of India." I placed it under my pillow before bed, believing in the power of intention. I prayed deeply, offering roses to the divine, and held onto the belief that if my intentions were pure, the universe would align.

There were moments of doubt, but I reminded myself to trust the process. Then, as if by divine intervention, everything fell into place. On August 15th, we received confirmation of our appointment. It was nothing short of a miracle.

Arriving at Rashtrapati Bhavan was a surreal experience. The palace stood majestic, its gardens pristine and vibrant. Memories of my childhood came rushing back. I recalled visiting Delhi with my father, who pointed to the grand building and said, "One day, you'll go inside." It felt as though this moment was written in the stars long ago.

The security was tight, but the staff's hospitality was warm and welcoming. When we entered her office, the President greeted us graciously. What I thought would be a brief meeting turned into a 45-minute conversation. She spoke about her journey and how my late father's teachings had influenced her life. This unexpected connection added a deeply personal touch to the encounter.

Walking through the palace gardens afterward, I couldn't help but marvel at how everything had aligned. The roses, prayers, and beliefs created a moment I would cherish forever.

## Conclusion

This journey taught me that dreams can become reality when fuelled by faith and persistence, no matter how improbable. The meeting with the President was more than just a proud moment; it was a reminder of the power of manifestation and the strength of family.

As I shared the story with my loved ones, their joy and pride mirrored my own. The experience reaffirmed my belief that the universe conspires to make the impossible possible when intentions are pure and rooted in goodness. Manifestation, combined with faith, action, and pure intentions, truly works. And this experience will forever remain one of the most cherished memories of my life.

# FROM VISION TO REALITY: HOW I BUILT THE LIFE I ALWAYS ENVISIONED

## BY MONIKA RAI

"*They* say dreams become a reality when passion meets determination, and I am living proof of that." Growing up in a Hindi-medium school, I was fascinated by the beauty of the English language. I worked relentlessly to attain fluency, fulfilling my aim of becoming an English trainer. I imagined myself delivering English-speaking classes, and this image fuelled a passion that drove all of my efforts in this direction.

I began enhancing my English skills, dedicating myself to expanding my vocabulary to an advanced level. However, I soon realised that my pronunciation wasn't perfect. Determined to improve, I invested in training with an American coach, who helped refine my accent and clarity.

Eager to put my knowledge into practice, I started recording videos on the English language and ventured into writing on Quora. This platform instantly captivated me with its vast reach—writers from over 80 countries shared their content here. I admired how top writers commanded respect; their words carried weight, and their comments and likes were valued immensely. They were like celebrities, inspiring thousands with powerful expressions and compelling narratives.

Although becoming a top writer seemed like an unattainable dream, I didn't let that discourage me. Instead, I dove deep into researching their writing styles to uncover what set them apart. I analysed their structure, tone, and formatting and incorporated these elements into my writing.

During my research, I discovered a crucial insight: Quora's algorithm favours long, detailed, and high-quality articles over sheer quantity. This realisation became my turning point.

I adjusted my writing strategy, crafting in-depth posts that provided real value to readers. The effort paid off—many of my articles went viral, reaching thousands worldwide. As my content gained traction, I transformed from just another contributor to a recognized name on Quora.

This platform didn't just amplify my reach; it cemented my identity as an English language expert. What started as a passion soon became a journey of influence and impact, and Quora became the stage where my voice truly resonated.

One morning, as I checked my notifications, my heart raced with excitement. Among the emails was a message that would change my life: Quora officials had informed me that I had been named the **Top Writer of 2018 in the English Language**. It felt surreal—a dream I had nurtured for years had finally come true.

From that moment, there was no looking back. As one of the select top writers, I was given the incredible opportunity to create my own space on Quora. That's how **"Fix Your English" was born—a space that now boasts over 200,000 followers and stands as one of the largest English language communities on the platform**.

Beyond Quora, I channelled my expertise into teaching, and training over a thousand adults in online spoken English and IELTS classes. Witnessing their transformation has been one of the most rewarding aspects of my journey.

Once I established myself as a writer on Quora, the desire to write a book took root in my heart. However, I soon realized that crafting blogs and articles was an entirely different journey compared to writing a full-length book. My mind was brimming with ideas, but choosing one to bring to life was no small task.

Every time I attended the annual International Book Fair, I would visualize myself not as a mere reader but as an author. The thought of seeing my book displayed among countless others ignited a fire within me—it was a dream that wouldn't let me rest and sleep. Fuelled by this vision, I began writing my first book. Despite my demanding schedule, I dedicated six to seven hours daily to my desk, pouring my heart and soul into my manuscript. I was so excited about my book that even late at night if a new idea struck me, I would immediately get up and start writing. There's something indescribable about watching your dream transform into reality, one word at a time. Seeing my book take shape was fulfilling.

In February 2024, my dream became a reality. I published my first book, both as an eBook and a paperback. To my utter joy, it was displayed at the World Book Fair in New Delhi. Words cannot capture the emotions I felt when I saw my book gracing the shelves of the fair's stalls. As I walked into the hall, there was an undeniable spring in my step. Watching readers pick up my book and make it their own was a surreal and deeply fulfilling experience. It was a moment of pure triumph, one that I will cherish forever.

## The Snowball Effect Of Daily Affirmations And Consistency

Since childhood, I have witnessed the power of small, consistent habits. **My father, Dr. S. B. Sinha,** diligently wrote his journal every day. Inspired by him, I picked up the same habit early on. But instead of merely documenting my day, I began scripting my future.

I filled my journal with affirmations like:

- "I speak English fluently."
- "I am a great public speaker."
- "I inspire others through my writing."

These were not just empty words; they were seeds I planted in my mind. Each affirmation reinforced my belief in my abilities and kept me aligned with my goals. Not once did I doubt my potential.

What followed was a journey of consistency and relentless effort. I stayed true to my vision, fuelled by positivity and determination. Slowly but surely, these small, actions began to snowball into tangible results. The energy I put into my affirmations and actions attracted opportunities, people, and circumstances that matched my goals.

I took another significant step towards self-improvement by removing all negative-minded people from my life. I unfollowed everyone who gave off negative vibes and failed to add value to my journey.

By focusing on positive energy, I realized I was not just creating a better mindset—I was shaping my reality. My dreams, which once seemed distant, started taking shape. Looking back, I can confidently say that everything in my life has been a result of this snowball effect. Your actions today might seem small, but with time, they can become the driving force behind the life you envision.

## About the Author

I'm Monika Rai, an IELTS & Language Trainer, Best Selling Author, Youtuber, and Quora Top Writer. I've helped more than a thousand students to gain fluency. Many of my students are English Trainers now. Through this anthology, I want to share how small daily affirmations coupled with consistent efforts and the hidden power of journaling transformed my dreams into reality.

# FROM DESPERATION TO MANIFESTATION: A JOURNEY OF TRANSFORMATION

## – BY BAJAN BOPANNA

*I*t was mid-October 2007, I was rushing towards my building in one of the beautiful campuses in Electronic City – Bangalore, when I was about to log in, there were others who were rushing to catch their cab/buses to reach home. It was a normal scene to me, as I was working in the so-called graveyard shift in a US-based process in

Bangalore, starting at 5 PM and ending at 2 AM. Despite completing a year at the job and working relentlessly, my mind was restless. Questions and doubts swirled incessantly. I kept replaying my life, trying to understand where things had gone wrong and how I could fix them.

Just a year earlier 2006, my life had seemed full of promise. Being selected by Infosys BPO during a campus interview felt like the beginning of something magical. My family was ecstatic. It wasn't just a celebration—it was a victory for all of us. News of my selection spread through our small town, and I became the centre of attention at every gathering. Relatives congratulated me, neighbours admired my success, and my parents beamed with pride.

I was equally excited. With ₹1500 in my pocket, a tiffin of home-cooked food, and a Coca-Cola bottle filled with boiled water (a middle-class cost-cutting hack), I boarded a government bus to Bangalore. My aunt accompanied me, offering advice along the way. She reminded me of the sacrifices my parents had made—pledging jewellery for my education, taking loans at high interest, and enduring hardships to see their son succeed. I listened intently, eager to absorb anything that could help me achieve my dreams faster.

But reality hit me like a storm. A year into my new life, the magic had vanished. My 4 digits salary, plus a meagre ₹40 per day night-shift allowance, barely helped me survive in Bangalore. Rent, food, credit card bills, personal loans, and postpaid bills left me penniless by the month's end. My CIBIL score had plummeted to 540, making banks refuse me outright.

As the eldest son, I carried the weight of my family's struggles. My father, who had lost a leg to amputation, couldn't work. My aunt, who lived with us, was mentally and physically challenged. My sister was pursuing college, and my younger brother, eight years junior, was still in school. My mother bore the burden of keeping the household running amidst these struggles.

The pressure was unbearable. I would stare at Excel sheets, trying to map out ways to clear private loans with heavy interest, pay EMIs, save for my sister's wedding, and build a house. Every calculation ended in despair. I felt trapped, as if life had me cornered.

When EXCEL failed me, I turned to WORD. During my graveyard shifts, I completed my work quickly and spent the remaining time pouring my thoughts into a document. I wrote about everything—my frustrations, my dreams, and the life I wished to live. I dreamed of building a home in Coorg with a horse at the gate, swings in the yard, and the kind of peace I had only imagined. I envisioned myself running a successful business, creating a routine that gave me control over my life.

On October 16, 2007, I emailed myself that Word document with the subject line: *"Home and Business Management—My Dream of Evergreen Sweet Home."* It wasn't just a document; it was my lifeline, my first attempt to manifest a life that seemed impossible.

That vision became my driving force. Despite my struggles, I held onto those dreams tightly. I started exploring every opportunity I could find. I joined professional dance groups, acted in TV serials, and even started small side businesses. I worked tirelessly, telling myself I wouldn't give up, no matter what.

Slowly, things began to change.

The universe responded to my energy and determination. My efforts multiplied, and opportunities began flowing in ways I couldn't have imagined. Today, those dreams that once felt like distant fantasies are my reality.

I now own an award-winning adventure resort in Coorg, a manifestation of the vision I nurtured back in 2007. My home, my family's well-being, my financial stability—all of it exceeds what I once dared to dream. The most magical part? What I've achieved isn't just what I envisioned; it's far greater.

Looking back, the journey feels like a miracle. But it wasn't easy. The years of desperation and relentless chasing often led me to the edge of depression. I learned the hard way that chasing dreams with desperation drains you. It wasn't until I aligned my energy with my vision—manifesting with purpose and clarity—that everything began to fall into place.

Now, I manifest with intention and work with boundless energy, making my life more exciting, fulfilling, and meaningful.

I am Bajan Bopanna—an actor by passion, the proud owner of a thriving business Evergreen County Adventure Retreat www.evergreencounty.com, a content creator, and a celebrity life coach for business owners. Since 2009, I've personally hosted over 100,000 guests at my resort. My mission now is to inspire and transform the lives of business owners, helping them master seven key areas of life and live like celebrities.

Through this story, I want to remind you that no matter how dire your circumstances, the power to change your life lies within you. Manifestation is real. When you combine your energy, emotions, and actions with a clear vision, the universe conspires to make it happen.

If I could rise from financial despair to build a multi-crore business and live a life of purpose and abundance, so can you.

Your dreams are valid, and your journey can be magical. Believe in it, work for it, and watch the miracles unfold. Through this anthology, I hope to inspire a lot of people to experience the magic in their own LIFE to get on TRACK they want to be in.

# MANIFESTING MAGIC

## BY ANU MALIK GARG

*I* turned fifty, and it felt like I had lived five lifetimes in the last five months while navigating the toughest phase of my life—battling a cancer journey with one of my closest family members.

My children packed me to Goa for a short break, to recharge. Numb, fatigued, exhausted, and scared I was sitting at the beach all alone just gazing, doing nothing trying to make sense of my emotions that kept crashing on the shore in tune with the restless noisy waves. My mind kept screaming silently competing with the seagulls aching to find my horizon with the sun as it raced towards oblivion.

My life was flashing before me in technicolour. The sudden realisation of immortality and how fleeting life is served as a jarring wake-up call. It was a moment where the woman in me woke up to take account of who I am, my achievements and what I want from myself in the next innings – and surprisingly I fell short of answers. During this process of rumination, as I mindlessly scribbled on the sand, I subconsciously wrote ***#freefifties***. I guess that was my manifestation.

When I scribbled #freefifties in the sand, I didn't realize I was planting a seed. In the days that followed, I began visualizing what 'free' truly meant to me—free from societal expectations, free from self-doubt, free to dream again. It was a deep desire to live my life post-fifties free from everything and just live it for myself. To dig out all the dreams and desires that I had packed up when life happened. It was time to dust them, air them and give them their due. That's when these intense conversations with myself began.

Out of the blue, my sister enrolled me in a poetry challenge. I started writing poems that became my catharsis – a journey of self-discovery and self-healing to reflect, recollect, reminisce, rejoice and recover. The process of

Journaling, writing poems, positive visualisations and affirmations became the everyday rituals that became my north star. I revelled in the chance to purge, reflect and give me that essential dose of positivity and peace that I craved the most.

The poems and prose that I tirelessly penned every day are a few slices of those intense intimate conversations, self-revelations, and memories bitter and sweet. It was a cleansing process of self-reflection, deep internalisation, and a journey of finding & forgiving myself and falling in love with myself all over again. Within three months I was a new person. Deeply inspired I started working on an interactive workshop for women in their fifties who were feeling lost & empty, menopausal, empty nesters who had forgotten who they were or their life's calling. To help them rediscover a new, confident, evolved self and explore the themes of self-love and healing.

A random advertisement of my coach Inspiring Jatin landed on my feed and my life changed. When he asked me what the book's name was, I said "Free Fifties." And that's how my first book Free Fifties was born, from a manifestation of a dream to be free and chase my dreams fearlessly to a best-selling author. It was as though the universe had aligned everything perfectly for that one meeting. My age-old dream of over 30 years of being an author came true within a day of meeting him.

And that's when it started sinking in - the power of manifestation. How the whole universe started planning it for me and I was unaware of it, till it actually happened. In hindsight, I can now connect the dots and see how the magic of manifestation worked behind the scenes to make my dream come true.

As I write this piece I am on a cruise, in Goa and it feels like life just came full circle. Sitting on the deck, watching the same ocean that once mirrored my inner turmoil, I felt a profound sense of gratitude. This wasn't just a vacation—it was a celebration of how far I had come. With limited time and almost no network, I am racing against time to share my story of magic and manifestation, dreams and determination, perseverance and purpose.

Manifestation isn't just about wishing; it's about aligning your thoughts, actions, and energy with your desires. Write down your dreams, visualize them vividly, and take small, consistent steps toward them. Today manifestation is my mantra. When I am at my highest I make a bigger wish and visualise that wish being fulfilled not once but many times and then I start working towards it. When I am at my lowest I do the same… many more times and work harder….with an immense faith that the universe is listening and spinning its magic. That I am not alone and there is a higher order watching, protecting, and guiding constantly.

My journey taught me that life doesn't end at fifty; it begins anew. The magic of manifestation is available to all of us if we dare to believe and act. So, what's your #freefifties moment? It's never too late to dream again.

## About the Author

Anu Malik Garg is a self-help advocate, a certified Design Thinking Trainer, and the author of multiple bestselling books. With her debut work, Free Fifties (an AMAZON #1 BESTSELLER), Anu has empowered countless women to embrace their authentic selves, rediscover their dreams, and embark on journeys of self-love and healing. Anu is on a mission to reach as many women as possible through her free workshops, encouraging them to rediscover their dreams, rebuild confidence, and embrace a happier, more fulfilled life.

Website- authoranugarg.com

Email - authoranugarg@gmail.com

Insta: freefities

# FROM ASPIRATION TO ACHIEVEMENT: A MANIFESTATION JOURNEY

## BY SURYANARAYANA S.V.

"*C*ongratulations! Excellent! That's fantastic!" My smartphone buzzed relentlessly with messages brimming with pride and admiration. I had just concluded a session at an international conference in Bangkok when this awesome moment came about. To be precise, it was Rotary International's 103rd Annual Convention 2012, an event that attracted over 25,000 Rotarian delegates from all corners of the globe. There, I fulfilled a long-held desire of mine.

The applause and cheers marked the culmination of a lifelong dream: to address a global audience and make an impact that transcended borders. This changed into no normal accomplishment. For years, I had been waiting for this moment, weaving it into my aspirations as a Rotary volunteer and a passionate activist for career guidance.

My involvement with Rotary began in 1996. Rotary clubs, united worldwide, are called Rotary International. This global service organization and its members believe in the power of service as a means to attain fulfilment and happiness.

I organized and moderated, on behalf of Rotary, over 100 impactful career guidance projects across India and beyond. This has informally shaped me into the "Career Man." They include public seminars on numerous career options. My work garnered attention, not only from Rotary circles but also from students, parents, teachers, and the media. People responded positively to these public seminars, establishing me as a prominent figure. Rotary International (RI) noticed and acknowledged my work.

Yet, one dream remained unfulfilled: sharing my vision with a worldwide audience and making it accessible to an international viewership.

I spent months crafting my signature presentation, "We Walk With Youth," as the founder and president of India's first Rotary eClub. Little did I recognize that this dream—rooted in purpose and fuelled by unwavering belief—was getting ready to manifest.

## Turning desires into possibilities

I aimed to reach a global target audience to encourage and empower young people, drawing from years of career guidance experience. Rotary International started allowing proposals for breakout sessions by various Rotary Clubs at its grand annual convention. RI leaders now oversee a competitive application process, which has become a challenge.

I meticulously crafted my application, detailing my successes and the impact of my career projects, while battling self-doubt about its quality. After weeks of anticipation, I received the acceptance email, becoming one of the few from India chosen to present a breakout session.

This journey affirmed my commitment and showed that willpower can conquer challenges and self-doubt.

## Making It Happen: The Big Day

I obtained my visa, finalized my itinerary, and secured shared accommodation in Bangkok, feeling elated and grateful for my dream adventure. This achievement was the result of months of hard work, focusing on intention, visualization, and perception.

I practiced visualization every day, imagining myself optimistically addressing a worldwide target audience, listening to applause, and feeling the audience's connection to my words. This practice reinforced my belief that my dream could become reality.

Upon arriving in Bangkok, the coordination of activities felt magical. Norah Webster, the RI officer, welcomed us with meticulous planning and enthusiasm. Promotional materials prominently featured our session, serving as a reminder of the event's significance.

Norah Webster and her crew attended to every detail, making sure of flawless organization. On the day of the presentation, I collaborated with friends and esteemed panellists, including Rtn. Sambasiva Rao (Sam), the former governor of Rotary District 3150, Rtn. Srinivasa Rao, the president of the Rotary Club of Hyderabad East, and Rtr. Thansen Paandi, the president of Rotaract South Asia, the youth wing of Rotary International, who meticulously reviewed our session outline.

I felt a deep connection to our subject matter, "We Walk With Youth," which converted from a presentation into a challenge.

When the scheduled time finally arrived, the energy in the conference hall was exciting. Our presentation flowed seamlessly, and we connected with the target audience, igniting their enthusiasm.

Reflecting on this journey, it showcased how purpose and persistence can align. From the opportunity to present, every moment felt like a perfect blend of effort, perception, and luck at every step.

## Celebrating Success: What Manifestation Taught Me

As I stepped out of the hall after completing the 2-hour breakout session, Norah approached me with a warm smile. "Congratulations, Surya," she stated, "for delivering a well-structured breakout session."

Her phrases filled me with pride and satisfaction. However, her next statement resonated deeply with me. She defined that unique practice of recognizing everybody who has contributed to my journey through signed certifications.

This understanding played a crucial role in my selection for the breakout session opportunity. She additionally discovered that I had embodied the spirit of Rotary service—giving back with gratitude and acknowledgment.

I learned a lot from this experience. Manifestation, in my opinion, is about encouraging others in addition to achieving one's very own dreams.

Gratitude and acknowledgment have a cumulative impact. It opens up opportunities that we won't have previously taken into consideration, much like the one I experienced. By valuing the contributions of others, we align ourselves with strength and possibility.

Putting purpose, gratitude, and inspired action together can lead to unexpected responses from the world.

## About the Author

I am Suryanarayana S.V., a veteran corporate consultant who became a celebrated author with over 45 years of global experience. From teenage achievement to international impact, the journey reflects a passion for writing, coaching, and speaking on self-improvement and career advancement. I am an Amazon bestselling author of "Career Boost: Nine Certification Advantages." I have contributed to two world-record achievements with the International Council of Authors.

Through this anthology, I aim to continue inspiring my readers and clients with my writing, coaching, and speaking engagements. My non-fiction self-improvement books and articles on various topics serve as a source of inspiration and a testament to my multifarious topic competency. Look up my catalogue, www.suryanarayana.in, containing an overview of my writings that have inspired readers worldwide, embodying service, creativity, and excellence. Explore more at http://www.suryanarayana.com

# FROM TRAUMA TO TRANSFORMATION: A JOURNEY OF SELF-DISCOVERY

## MY IDEAL BODY WEIGHT AND FITNESS TRANSFORMATION STORY

### BY DR. GAVESHANA SHROTRIYA

*T*wo years ago, when everything went wrong in my life. My mental, emotional and physical health was in the worst condition. I was going through so much (divorce, separation with my child and emotional trauma) .

Although I was a fitness professional, I struggled to reduce my postpartum weight with lots of health issues (blood pressure, thyroid, depression and insomnia) due to 5 years of difficult circumstances in my marriage.

When I did not find the right path. One opportunity and a call gave me hope.

It was a strong sign from the universe that the manifestation of my healthy and fit body was in the right direction.

## My Why .......

Achieving the ideal body weight and best shape was very crucial for me because before pregnancy I was in my best shape and enjoyed a fitness lifestyle already (a marathoner and certified group instructor).

Since pregnancy, I have faced lots of stressful situations and they were increasing day by day. Five years of these difficult circumstances impacted my health and fitness. I did reduce my weight and improved my fitness many times, but somehow, I was not consistent in the process due to my situation and I came back to my previous unhealthy state. A vicious cycle of weight reduction and gain was going on.

But when I separated from my child, that suffering was so painful for me that it not only affected my physical health but I lost my mental well-being as well.

Somehow the desire to be in the best shape and health was still burning in my heart.

At that time due to my financial situation, I searched for a job and I had the opportunity to work as a regional fitness manager and event head.

This was the first sign the universe gave me **(right environment)** and showed me that my manifestation was working.

As a fitness professional, I had to design fitness events for members so that they could improve their health and fitness and enjoy a healthy active lifestyle. At that moment I realized why not me, but the next moment I felt it was not possible for me in that situation. I saw a visual. I was in a deep dark pit and it seemed impossible to get out of that darkness. But in my heart, I strongly believed that only I can do what it takes to get out of this reality, I have to take this giant leap of faith and create a new version of myself.

It's my journey and only I can help myself. I recollected my past achievements and experiences. How a reserved sensitive doctor turned into a marathoner, group instructor and fitness coach. This insight changed my mind set and I manifested my ideal body weight and best-ever shape again.

## The journey of my TRANSFORMATION 2.0 Begins

To transform my health & fitness....Here is what I did:

Every day in the morning, I visualized myself as I already reached my ideal body weight and the best ever shape feeling healthy and happy.

Everybody is congratulating me and appreciating me. I acted as if I am fit and healthy. I aligned my thoughts, emotions and actions accordingly and followed my exercise and diet regime very seriously, fully accepting myself and showing gratitude for my health and fitness.

One day my previous coach and mentor called me and invited me to join his new and encouraging community where he helps people to transform their life and achieve ideal body weight. This was the second time **(Right mentor)** cosmos showed me the path.

It seemed to me that the universe has always been with me on the journey because due to my circumstances, I wasn't in touch with him for a very long time. What I had to do was just trust the process and go with the flow. It gave me more power and confidence to manifest my dream body and the rest is history.

After joining this community, not only did I achieve my ideal body weight but I also regained my health and fitness. I won the **Ideal Body Weight Trophy** (lost 22 kg weight and more than 30 + inches & free from all health issues) and **Fitness Icon Trophy.**

## Conclusion and lesson learned

This journey taught me that manifestation is not just about thinking but about taking inspired and desired action for achieving your goals with full faith and gratitude. When you surrender to the universe and trust the process everything comes to you in a magical way.

Manifestation is the bridge between where you are now and where you want to be. Because everything is present in the universe we just have to tap into this frequency. And it is possible only when you match your frequency to your desired reality.

So, combining the manifestation technique with consistent efforts and persistence is vital in achieving any goal.

## About the Author

I'm Dr. Gaveshana 2x best-selling author, homoeopathic doctor, dietician, certified fitness coach, marathoner, wellness and mindset coach. With a passion for transforming people's lives by sharing my knowledge and wisdom and helping people to live a blissful life despite whatever challenges they have faced.

Through this anthology, I want to inspire people that everything is possible – **"if one man can do another can too"**.

Focus on thriving, not only surviving, even in your darkest time. Nothing is impossible, because you are the creator of your life. So, believe in your dreams and turn them into reality.

# MANIFESTING THE LIFE YOU DESIRE: A PERSONAL JOURNEY OF BELIEF AND TRANSFORMATION

## BY SUSHIL GROVER

*I* come from a humble background, losing both my parents at just two years old. As the youngest, I was raised by my grandparents with my two older brothers and sister. I never understood my purpose in this world. What is manifestation, and how can it bring a profound shift in my life?

Manifestation is the belief that by focusing on our desires with unwavering faith, we can attract the people, opportunities, and resources to make them real. It is about aligning our energy with our goals, not wishful thinking. This chapter shares my journey, showing how belief and action lead to extraordinary change.

For as long as I can remember, I dreamed of working in a prestigious organization where I could make a significant impact. I was 16 years old when I first passed by a towering building on the Ring Road in New Delhi. My brother was driving the scooter, and as we passed this majestic building, I thought to myself, "Who are the people who work here? If I were to work here, it would be amazing." At the time, it seemed like an impossible dream—one that belonged to others. But fast forward to adulthood, and there I was, working at that very building—The Oberoi, a five-star hotel in New Delhi—for five transformative years. That moment made me realize how powerful my thoughts were. What once seemed like a far-fetched fantasy had turned into a reality.

This was just the beginning. As I focused more on my aspirations, I began noticing opportunities I had never seen before. Visualization alone, however, was not enough. I also kept a gratitude journal, where I expressed thanks for the opportunities I had not yet received but knew were on their way. I allowed myself to feel the emotions of success and fulfilment, as if they were already part of my reality.

However, there were times when my belief in manifestation was truly tested. One such instance was during my preparation for competitive exams. I had applied to numerous job vacancies—from government exams to bank positions. One day, I went to a bank to get a draft made for my exam fee. As I watched the cashier process my payment, the voucher passed through various hands—first the peon, then the clerk, and the supervisor—until it reached the Branch Manager, who signed it effortlessly before leaning back in his chair. At that moment, I thought, "I want that job. I want to be the one signing papers like that." Just a few years later, I found myself working as a Branch Manager in a public-sector bank.

This was another clear example of how manifestation works. When you desire something with all your heart, the universe aligns to help you. As I remained focused on my intentions, the opportunities I needed began to materialize. The belief that got me that prestigious job also helped me navigate my career through challenges.

One such challenge occurred during a quarterly performance review meeting. I had to present the performance of my branch in front of the Chief Regional Manager and 50 other Branch Managers. When it was my turn, I was publicly scolded for something that was not my fault. I felt humiliated in front of my peers. But instead of feeling defeated, I told myself, "One day, people like you will attend my leadership and soft skills sessions." It was a vision I held onto despite the situation. A few years later, I became a senior faculty member and delivered leadership training sessions to senior leaders, including those under whom I had once worked.

Reflecting on my journey, I realize that manifestation is not just about visualizing a dream or asking the universe for what you want. It is about aligning your thoughts, emotions, and actions to the belief that your dreams are already on their way. Trusting the process, I began attracting the right opportunities at the right time. This experience taught me that the energy we put out into the world profoundly impacts what we attract.

The lessons I learned from manifesting my dreams go beyond career success. I now understand the true power of belief—that when you commit wholeheartedly to your goal, the universe begins to rearrange itself to bring that goal closer to you. I encourage you to trust the manifestation process in your life. With faith, belief, and consistent action, the universe will help you bring your dreams to reality. Every time you take inspired action and maintain a positive, focused mindset, you draw yourself closer to your goals.

In conclusion, manifestation is not merely about wishing for things to happen. It is about actively aligning your thoughts, emotions, and actions with a clear, focused vision of what you want to achieve. As I reflect on my own journey, I am amazed by how belief, visualization, and persistent action have shaped my life. I encourage you to embrace the power of manifestation in your journey—remain focused, believe in yourself, and take purposeful actions. The universe will begin to work in your favour, bringing the opportunities, resources, and people necessary to make your dreams a reality.

By trusting the manifestation process, you can create a life that feels aligned with your deepest desires, just as I did in my own journey. Let the universe conspire to help you achieve your goals.

## About the Author

### Sushil Grover

*Author, Leadership Coach, Mentor, and Soft Skills Trainer*

Through this chapter, I aim to spread the message that each individual is unique and capable of achieving anything in life. Coming from a modest background myself, I have gone on to become an author, leadership coach, mentor, and soft skills trainer, impacting hundreds of lives. If I, with my humble beginnings, could turn my dreams into reality, I truly believe anyone can achieve his dreams.

# THE SECRET INGREDIENT THAT HELPED ME MANIFEST IN SECONDS!

## BY JUHI DAMODAR

*L*ast year, I completed my professional course on Handwriting Analysis and Grapho-Therapy, earning an impressive 4.5-star rating. However, I was just one step away from mastering the final level of knowledge I needed. The expectations from those familiar with my journey were high, and it felt disheartening to consider giving up right before achieving complete success due to financial constraints. With no desire to take out loans and an aversion to seeking help, I wished for a miracle. Little did I know, the universe was listening to my deepest desires.

My aspiration to complete the Master's course went beyond just acquiring knowledge; it was also about establishing an alternate source of income. So much was riding on this opportunity. After moving from a bustling metropolitan area to a Tier-2 city to fulfil my father's dream, he passed away unexpectedly just months later. This loss led to numerous internal family conflicts, leaving me in a place with little growth or income. My savings were dwindling, and societal norms often equated success with financial stability. It's easy to let emotions cloud our judgment, but I was proud to have honoured my father's last wish. Now, I had no choice but to confront my fears and overcome the odds—I was not about to give up.

Recognizing that I was physically alone but supported by the blessings and guidance of a greater power, I was determined to succeed. I had a strong intuition that financial support would come my way, though I had no idea from where or how. My journey of spiritual growth led me to meditate and practice Sadhanas for five continuous years. I embraced gratitude, but I hadn't fully realized that I was not alone in this journey. I had been somewhat lazy about practicing manifestations, doubting that I could truly create unexpected outcomes. After all, if manifesting were that easy, everyone would simply manifest their desires instead of putting in hard work. I knew many shared this scepticism.

Whenever I entered a meditative state, it felt like stepping into a different world—one free of negative thoughts and full of surrender. In this deep state of relaxation, fresh ideas would often flow in. One day, I felt compelled to explore the concept of manifestation. I read a few books, but my belief in its effectiveness was still shaky.

The turning point came when I was informed that I needed to make the payment for my Master's degree. That same day, a strong desire for money surged within me. I decided to harness that feeling to begin my manifestation practice. I settled into meditation, closed my eyes, and focused on visualizing my desires. Almost immediately, I heard a text notification on my phone. Normally, I wouldn't have opened my eyes during meditation, but something compelled me to do so. Without even glancing at the message, I somehow knew it wasn't spam; it was about the money I needed.

When I opened the text, I was stunned to discover that a family member—someone who had never before offered me assistance—had deposited the exact amount I required into my account. This was crazy! Unbelievable! How can that happen just like that? I had never asked anyone for it other than the universe. Then I truly understood the saying "Kehte hain ki, agar kisi cheez ko dil se chaaho to puri kayanaat usey tumse milane ki koshish mein lag jaati hai" (meaning if you wish for something from your heart, then the whole universe conspires to get it for you). This experience taught me that manifestation involves more than just techniques and visualization; it requires a deep, genuine desire for what you want. If our minds are cluttered with negativity, manifestation becomes nearly impossible.

I want to share this with anyone who believes that manifestation is unrealistic, merely a form of toxic positivity or a passing trend. Manifestation is a powerful key to embracing optimism and recognizing the existence of a greater force that defies scientific explanation. It is as real as you are!

## About the Author

I am **Juhi Damodar**, Advocate, Author, Researcher, President of the Child Welfare Committee, Internationally Certified Handwriting Analyst and Grapho Analytical Therapist, Master Practitioner of Graphology, Winning participant of the prestigious World Record with the International Council of Authors, Parental Alienation, and Animal Rights activist, Animal Lover, Meditator with a passion for spiritual development and manifestation. Through this anthology, I hope to inspire others to accept, that there is a greater magical power existing in the universe beyond scientific explanation.

# FROM HUMBLE BEGINNINGS TO GLOBAL SUCCESS: MY MANIFESTATION JOURNEY

## BY SUJOY CHOWDHURY

Success is often perceived as a destination, but for me, it has been a transformative journey. What makes my story special is the role that manifestation played in turning my dreams into reality. From starting with zero capital to building a thriving business with offices and networks spanning across India, Australia, Canada, UK, USA, and Dubai, my journey is a testament to the power of belief, determination, and hard work. I started my company Sc

Overseas Consultancy Services Pvt Ltd (known as OCS Kolkata) with a vision to help students achieve success abroad.

## The Beginning: A Vision without Resources

I started with nothing but a dream. There were no funds to back my aspirations, no office to work from, and no established network to lean on. However, I had a clear vision of what I wanted to achieve, helping students make their dream careers abroad. This vision was my driving force, and it kept me motivated even in the face of countless challenges.

## The Power of Manifestation

Manifestation became my guiding principle. I would visualize my goals as if they were already accomplished. I imagined myself running a successful business, empowering students, and creating opportunities for them worldwide. Every time I faced a roadblock, I reminded myself that the universe aligns with those who are persistent and purposeful. Manifestation wasn't just about dreaming; it was about aligning my thoughts, actions, and energy with my goals.

I also used manifestation to build a fulfilling life for my family. I visualized a life of joy, abundance, and togetherness. Over time, my family and I were able to travel the world, experiencing new cultures and creating unforgettable memories. Manifestation allowed me to strike a balance between professional success and personal happiness, ensuring that my family's dreams were intertwined with mine.

## The Desire to Create Change

The desire to create change in the lives of students was the spark that ignited my journey. I wanted to bridge the gap between dreams and reality for those aspiring to study and work abroad. This desire grew stronger with every student I interacted with. Each conversation revealed unique challenges, and my determination to provide solutions became the cornerstone of my mission.

## Building from Zero

Starting with no capital meant I had to be resourceful. I began small, working from home and leveraging every opportunity to connect with students and professionals. Slowly but surely, word spread about the quality of services I provided. Each success story added to my credibility and gave me the confidence to expand further.

## The Journey of Growth

My journey has been one of consistent learning and adapting. Every milestone, whether big or small, brought new insights and experiences. As the business grew, I embraced challenges as opportunities to innovate and improve. Expanding into new cities and countries required courage, but the thought of helping more students fuelled my efforts. The journey was not just about professional growth, it was also about personal transformation. I became more resilient, empathetic, and focused as I navigated the complexities of building a global network. Every day, numerous students visit our website ([www.ocsedu.com](www.ocsedu.com)) to book free online counselling sessions and connect with our certified counsellors for expert guidance at no cost.

## Manifesting Student Success

Manifestation extended beyond my personal and professional life. I began to manifest success for the students I worked with. Every time a student approached me with their aspirations, I visualized their dreams coming true. I would see them walking into their dream universities, thriving in their chosen careers, and creating a better future for themselves and their families. This mindset not only motivated me but also created a positive energy that inspired the students to believe in themselves.

## Manifestation Practices

Manifestation isn't magic; it's a process that involves intention, belief, and action. Here are some practices that worked for me:

1. **Visualization**: I dedicated time daily to visualize my goals as if they were already accomplished.
2. **Affirmations**: Positive affirmations reinforced my belief in my abilities and the universe's support.
3. **Gratitude**: I consistently expressed gratitude for what I had and for the success I was manifesting.
4. **Action**: Manifestation requires action. I aligned my efforts with my goals, ensuring every step brought me closer to success.

## Growth and Expansion

As my business grew, so did my aspirations. What started as a one-person operation has now expanded to a network with a presence in almost every major city in India and internationally in Australia, Canada, UK, USA, and Dubai. This growth wasn't accidental, it was the result of strategic planning, relentless effort, and a commitment to excellence.

## Impact: Changing Lives

The most fulfilling part of my journey has been the impact I have had on others. Over the years, I have helped more than 10,000 students achieve their dreams of studying and building careers abroad. Each success story reminds me of why I started this journey. Seeing their lives transform and knowing that I played a role in their success is the greatest reward.

## Lessons Learned

1. **Believe in Yourself**: No matter how big the dream is, self-belief is the foundation of success.
2. **Manifestation Works**: When you align your thoughts and actions with your goals, the universe responds.
3. **Hard Work is Irreplaceable**: Manifestation sets the direction, but hard work propels the journey.
4. **Gratitude Magnifies Results**: Being thankful amplifies positive energy and attracts more success.
5. **Resilience is Key**: Challenges are inevitable, but perseverance makes the difference.

## The Future

While I am proud of how far I have come, I believe this is just the beginning. My goal is to continue expanding my network, helping more students achieve their dreams, and inspiring others to believe in the power of manifestation.

My journey from an ordinary person to a life I once only dreamed of is proof that success is possible for anyone willing to work for it. Manifest your dreams, stay committed, and let your actions speak louder than your doubts. The life you desire is within reach, you just have to believe.

# A PEN AND A VISION

## BY JAPJOT KANG

Two years ago, I felt lost in a sea of wellness coaches. The market was saturated with seasoned experts, leaving me questioning whether I could ever stand out. Could I genuinely make an impact? One restless evening, as I scrolled through social media, I stumbled upon an advertisement that would change everything. It was simple yet profound – nine letters that resonated with my deepest aspiration: AUTHORITY. Something ignited within me. That moment became the turning point in my journey, unlocking a hidden potential I hadn't realised I possessed.

In just 11 months, I authored six books, each reflecting the tools I used to overcome chronic anxiety and develop emotional resilience. These books became my voice and platform and answered a question I'd been pondering: How can I share my methods with the world and become a trusted authority in my field? The transformation was nothing short of extraordinary.

For years, I wrestled with the weight of anxiety. I tried everything - online resources and anti-anxiety medications – but nothing seemed to offer the relief I so desperately needed. Each method promised change, but none provided a quick, effective, or lasting solution. The frustration of feeling stuck and helpless was overwhelming, and it led me to a pivotal moment: if the answers didn't exist, then I would have to create them myself.

That's when I stumbled upon Neuro-Linguistic Programming (NLP) and mindfulness. What began as a simple curiosity turned into a transformative revelation. By combining these tools to suit my needs, I created a unique approach that didn't just offer temporary relief—it changed my emotional state in days, not months. The results were nothing short of phenomenal. I had found the breakthrough I had been searching for and couldn't keep it to myself. I knew then that my mission was clear: to share this life-changing method with the world so others could experience the same freedom and resilience I had.

But the path wasn't without its doubts. In the beginning, I felt hopeless and stuck. I questioned whether I was truly capable of pursuing this journey. Should I continue forging independently, or would it be wiser to seek external guidance? In a moment of clarity, I decided to trust the process and work with a book-writing mentor who had already walked the path I was attempting to follow. This decision was a game-changer. I began to understand the profound value of mentorship – having someone to guide me toward success.

Writing became my outlet. It was my way of turning knowledge into action, transforming the tools and insights that had reshaped my life into something tangible for others. Although the writing process was sometimes overwhelming initially, it aligned perfectly with my lifelong passion for uplifting others. Sharing my journey and lessons through written words felt nothing short of magical. This journey taught me that our greatest struggles often hold the keys to our most profound purpose. For me, anxiety was a teacher in disguise. It led me to discover my true calling: uplifting, empowering, and inspiring others to break free from emotional turmoil. It all began with a single desire – to heal myself and, in doing so, help others rise.

Two years ago, my manifestation journey began with a unique practice I call The Genie Exercise. This technique utilises the Reticular Activating System (RAS), often called the brain's inner genie. The RAS filters out unnecessary information and prioritises what aligns with our goals. For instance, once you decide to buy a red car, you suddenly start noticing red cars everywhere. The RAS connects intention to action, turning desires into reality when consistently focused upon.

The exercise itself is simple yet profound. Each night, I wrote my intention 11 times in the present tense as if it had already come true. I began with two deep breaths, chanted "FOCUS" five times, and then read my intention aloud. I concluded by thanking my RAS three times, expressing gratitude for its role in helping me recognise opportunities to fulfil my desire.

Within weeks, I noticed signs—such as a shift in the advertisements I encountered, including clarity sessions, coaching programs, and personal growth workshops. The pivotal moment came when I discovered an ad that promised the fastest way to establish oneself as an authority in a field. By becoming an author, "authority" contains the word "author" within its first five letters. The synchronicity was unmistakable, and this leap of faith led me to a transformational journey.

This decision unlocked potential I hadn't realised I possessed. In just 11 months, I authored six books on my passion for emotional resilience and mental wellness.

Every step reinforced my belief that persistence and faith in our intentions create momentum. Just as Rome wasn't built in a day, and one can't expect to see visible changes in their body after a single gym session, our manifestations develop similarly, layer by layer and inch by inch. Strong beliefs pave the way for new outcomes, while weak beliefs hinder progress. The formula is straightforward: new intentions fuel new evidence, which, in turn, manifests new realities. Trust the process, and watch your vision come to life. I want to conclude with my quote.

"To consider something to be true or not to be true for you is up to you."

## About the Author

I am Japjot Kang, a bestselling author, NLP Master Practitioner, Mental and Emotional Wellness Coach, and multi-time winning world record participant. A smile generator and hope creator, I am passionate about making emotional wellness handy through my books and coaching skills. I sincerely believe in the power of intentional living. Through this anthology, I aspire to inspire others to embrace their potential and lead purposeful lives.

# MANIFESTATION GONE WRONG

## THE PERILS OF CALLING DARKNESS INTO YOUR LIFE

## BY ANSHU JOSHI SINGH

*"Manifestation is a double-edged whisper of the soul—what you summon isn't always light. Dreams and darkness answer your call, so tread carefully, for even the heart's quietest shadows can create storms."*

### Manifesting My Best and Worst Thoughts

I have often thought about the power of our thoughts and their manifestation in our lives. Do they shape our reality? My life's journey has been a testament to this mysterious force, showcasing its beauty and potential for devastation. I have seen my deepest fears come to life, but I have also experienced the miraculous realisation of my dreams.

I used to visit my cousin sisters on the outskirts of our town occasionally, and each time, the journey felt special—not because of the destination, but because of something I'd see on the way.

There was this beautiful little cottage by the road. It wasn't grand or imposing but magical—a tiny house adorned with flowers. Every time I passed it, I couldn't help but stare, imagining myself in a home like that someday. Without realising it, the words "I will have this kind of house one day" became a part of my routine, a quiet mantra I repeated often.

I didn't know who lived there, and it didn't seem necessary. Years later, I met someone in my circle of friends—a gentleman. As the months passed, our connection grew. Then, one day, while talking about life and childhood, he mentioned where he lived. It felt like time stopped for a moment when I realised that house—that cottage I had admired and dreamt of for so long—was *his*.

It was as if all the pieces of my life had fallen perfectly into place. That house had brought me to him, or maybe it was him who had always been tied to my dreams. The definition was not clear, but the concept was. I manifested that house, or did I manifest my husband with that house? The mystery still prevails.

## The Worst – A Manifestation of Fear

It began with fear—an all-consuming, gnawing anxiety that took root the day my younger brother, Amit, joined the army. He was our pillar of strength, filling our home with laughter and warmth. Yet, his decision to serve our country planted a seed of dread in my heart. Every headline about a conflict, every late-night phone call, sent a chill down my spine.

I tried to bury the fear, masking it with prayers and forced smiles, but it grew insidiously, feeding on my sleepless nights and silent tears. My thoughts became a worry loop: *What if something happens to him? What if we lose him?* I didn't realise then that the energy of my thoughts was weaving its way into reality.

The day the news arrived, our world crumbled. Amit had been martyred in a cross-border skirmish at the world's highest battlefield, the mighty Siachen. The weight of my fear manifested into an unbearable truth. I remember the moment with piercing clarity—the uniformed officers at the door, the look in their eyes, the words that shattered my soul. My fear had come alive, leaving a void in my heart that no words could fill.

For weeks, I lived in a haze of grief and guilt, convinced that my thoughts had brought this tragedy upon us. The vibrant person I once was had faded into a shadow. Losing Amit was the worst moment of my life, not just because he was gone, but because it felt like I had willed it into existence.

Looking back, I see the undeniable connection between my thoughts and reality. Fear consumed me and led to my darkest moment, while hope lifted me to my brightest. **Manifestation isn't magic; it's the energy we carry, our focus on our emotions, and our actions aligning with them.**

I've learned to be mindful of my thoughts, nurture those who empower me, and confront those who don't. The journey hasn't been easy, but it's been worth it. In all its complexity, Manifestation has shaped me into who I am today: a survivor, creator, and believer in the power of thought.

### The Best – Rising from Ashes

Years later, life dealt me another cruel hand. My business, which I had poured my heart into, collapsed spectacularly. It felt like I had lost everything: my savings, my reputation, and my sense of purpose. I spiralled into despair, wondering if life had anything left to offer me.

But amidst the wreckage, a tiny, stubborn ember of hope glowed. Amit's words came back to me: *"You're stronger than you think, Didi. Even if the world falls apart, you'll find a way to rebuild."* His voice, etched into my memory, became my guiding light.

I began to write—not with a goal, but simply to pour out the storm of emotions within me. Words became my sanctuary, each page a step toward healing. Gradually, my sorrow found form, transforming into stories that connected with others. Taking that leap was terrifying, but it was also exhilarating.

Although my desire to write and share my story was strong, the path felt unclear. That's when I stumbled upon an online coach. It was almost as if the universe had aligned to guide me. With his encouragement, my first book took shape. It wasn't perfect, but it was authentic and resonated deeply with readers.

I became an author, carving out an identity I never knew I had within me. Losing Amit taught me that life is fragile, but it also showed me the strength of the human spirit. Becoming an author wasn't just about writing books; it manifested my best thoughts; it was about reclaiming myself, proving that we can find a way to rise even in the face of unimaginable loss.

"Manifestation is the mirror of your soul, reflecting not only your dreams but your doubts, fears, and darkness. Be careful what you call forth, for not all those answers will bring light." It's a power-use wisely.

# MANIFESTING WHOLENESS: A JOURNEY OF HEALING AND TRANSFORMATION

## BY VIJAY SINGLA

*"Manifestation wasn't just a practice for me—it was a powerful journey that healed my body, calmed my mind, and transformed my life in ways I never imagined."*

*I* am Dr.(Mrs.) Vijay Singla from Chandigarh. I hold qualifications in B.Ed, M.Ed, NDDY, and P.G. (Advanced) NDDY. I am a Senior Faculty at the Art of Living, where I teach and guide individuals through various programs.

As a Healerpreneur and Counsellor, my passion lies in helping people find balance, healing, and peace through different modalities. My work is dedicated to empowering others and nurturing their well-being.

Manifestation brings something into your life through thoughts, feelings, and beliefs. It involves focusing your mental and emotional energy on a specific desire or outcome and believing it is possible. You can attract and create your desired reality by aligning your thoughts and feelings with your goals.

Manifestation practices often include visualisation, positive affirmations, goal setting, and the law of attraction. By maintaining a positive mindset and focusing on your wants, you can influence the universe or your subconscious mind to bring those things to fruition.

Simply put, Manifestation is the public display of emotion, feeling, or something.

I was raised in a very reputable family, provided with all the comforts and happiness of life. My life was full of abundance. As fate would have it, things were not the same after I got married. At times, it was even difficult to arrange food for my children. There was no support, not even from my husband. The major setback in my life was the demise of my father, which pushed me into depression—suffering for a long time on various fronts like physical and mental health, financial issues, children problems and a lot more. That was when god took mercy on me, and I happened to meet someone who took me to the Art of Living program. That is where I learned the method and tested the power of manifestation when I struggled with physical stiffness—my body was so tight that I found it hard to move, sit, or stand comfortably. Through manifestation, I regained my physical shape, allowing me to move easily and even enjoy exercise once more. This transformation has been a reminder of the power of focused intention and belief in achieving wellness.

On an emotional level, I've experienced a remarkable shift. I now have greater control over my emotions and feel more balanced and relaxed. I am calmer, more settled, and at peace. This sense of contentment has brought me happiness and a deep understanding of fulfilment in my life. It's as if I've learned to embrace each day with a sense of calm and serenity that was once elusive.

I manifested improved relations with my daughter. She was a hard person to deal with. My connection with others has also significantly improved. My relationship with my daughter has become much healthier and more harmonious. The positive changes in my emotional well-being have allowed me to approach relationships with greater patience, understanding, and love.

Manifestation has also made a tangible financial difference. I had been trying to sell a plot of land for five years and failed. After focusing on my desires through manifestation, it was finally sold. Additionally, I faced difficulties with a tenant who wouldn't vacate my flat. After applying the principles of manifestation, the tenant moved out, and I regained control over my property. These experiences have shown me the impact of positive energy and intention in attracting favourable outcomes.

On a spiritual level, manifestation has elevated my energy and deepened my meditation practice. I am more enthusiastic about my spiritual journey and feel more connected to my inner self and the universe. This heightened awareness has allowed me to explore deeper dimensions of my spirituality, finding peace and purpose in every moment.

Finally, my communication skills have also grown significantly. I can now express my thoughts, feelings, and emotions clearly and effectively. This ability to communicate with confidence and empathy has helped me connect better with others, whether in personal relationships or my work as a healer and counsellor. My communication skills have significantly developed, allowing me to express my thoughts, feelings, and emotions clearly and effectively. To achieve these benefits, I regularly engage in the following modules: Aura cleansing and energising, Seven chakra cleansing and energising, Panchkosha cleansing and energising, and the 5*55*5 technique."

Manifestation has transformed my physical, emotional, and financial well-being and enriched my spiritual and interpersonal lives. It's a journey of self-discovery and empowerment that allows me to live a more fulfilling and balanced life.

# FROM DREAMS TO BEST SELLERS

## MY MANIFESTATION JOURNEY
## A JOURNEY OF RESILIENCE, VISION, AND SUCCESS

### BY RASHMI K.

## Introduction

In 2020, I had a dream: to write a book and make it an Amazon bestseller. It sounded far from possible at that time since I didn't know where or how to start. Yet, every day, I wrote this dream in my goals, willing it into existence. Later joining one such workshop acted as the trigger to a chain of events and I was able to create two best-sellers, a dream far beyond my own belief system about my capabilities.

## Desire and the Journey

It was not just about seeing my name on the cover of a book; it was about satisfying a long-cherished dream and inspiring others to chase their dreams. But at that time, I was enthusiastic, yet life had different plans. I had a challenging job and some personal problems, which would frequently leave me stuck and unsure of where to start.

Well, all that changed when I came across a video by Inspiring Jatin. His energy and advice resonated so strongly with me that I bought his 3-day workshop. On the second day, I did something very out of character for me on social media: I announced to the world that I was writing a book titled "From Piggy Bank To Portfolio" and would be releasing it as an eBook in just one month. Terrifying and exhilarating was forcing myself into action, come what may, by making the commitment to the world.

Soon after, Jatin announced the ICA World Record attempt to publish the maximum number of eBooks in English for nonfiction. The deadline was August 6th, and it fit my schedule perfectly. But then I decided to stretch myself to attempt another book for the record, too. The pressure was immense. Writing, editing, and formatting two books at once-especially with my limited technical skills-was overwhelming.

The challenges did not end there. Life had more curveballs, and I lost my job, which left me in a very vulnerable place in life. There came phases of self-doubt and times when it seemed the only way out was to give up. But then, I remembered why I started. So, I refocused myself, dividing each day: one book in the morning, the other at night. And with time, little by little, I progressed. Each small thing, like completing the writing of a chapter or formatting a section, motivated me to forge ahead.

## The Process of Manifestation

The manifestation wasn't only about writing down my goals, but it had to be about aligning my activities with my intentions. I would visualize every morning how my books were topping the list of bestsellers. How people were getting benefits out of my words, and their parents teaching kids financial concepts through my guidebook; this kept me going even on the toughest days.

I relied on tools such as visualization, daily affirmations, and a great support system. The ICA community became my backbone, offering guidance and encouragement every step of the way. When I struggled with book cover designing or formatting, fellow members stepped in to help. Their unwavering support made the impossible seem possible.

On August 3rd, I received news that changed everything. The deadline for the ICA World Record was extended to August 28th. This gave me the extra time I was desperately in need of. Still, more than 14 hours on my computer day in and day out, I worked. Even though these were slow and foreign with software and new tools introduced to me like Canva, I kept going forward. Late nights became regular as I worked into details, perfecting everything from the structure in my chapters to just how my book covers would be designed.

Publishing both of them was a mountain hike. On the 13th of August, I submitted my pre-order request for the ICA book. On 28th August, after a tough wait, my books went live on the market. Seeing my book listed on Amazon was a shock, but later seeing it attain #1 and #2 best-selling positions felt more like my dream had been fulfilled. Much later, all I could remember was pride and an overwhelming feeling of gratitude towards God.

## Conclusion and Lessons Learned

This journey taught me that manifestation isn't magic—it's a blend of vision, action, and persistence. Writing my books and seeing them succeed reaffirmed my belief in the power of setting clear goals and trusting the process. Challenges are inevitable, but they're also opportunities to grow and prove to ourselves what we're capable of.

Another key lesson was the importance of community. Having a support system like ICA made all the difference, turning moments of doubt into opportunities for growth. Finally, I learned to celebrate every milestone, no matter how small, because they are the stepping stones to achieving bigger dreams. If I can turn my dreams into reality, so can you. The key is to start and never give up, no matter how daunting the journey may seem.

## About the Author

I am Rashmi K., an architect turned career coach and bestselling author. With over 20 years of experience, I empower young minds to achieve their dreams through practical skills and personal growth. My books, *"From Piggy Bank To Portfolio"* and *"21 Days To Go Beyond Routine"*, reflect my passion for teaching and inspiring others to manifest their ideal lives. I hope my story encourages you to take the first step toward your dreams.

# THE DREAM THAT REFUSED TO DIE

## BY RUCHIKA BHASKER

*S*itting on a lonely bench in Sector 17, Chandigarh, I felt the weight of the world pressing on me. The tears rolling down my cheeks, warmed by grief but chilled by the cold breeze, told a story I never imagined living. As I sat there, staring into nothingness, I thought: Is this how my life will proceed now? How had it come to this point? How far I had drifted from the dreams I once held so close. I was only 20, searching for stability and purpose in all the wrong places. A year back, life was a canvas painted with vibrant hues of joy. I was the best student, and the best daughter, until everything shattered in a single moment.

September 2009. The day my mother, my pillar of strength, left this world in a tragic accident and my life split into a before and an after. I lost not just my mother but also my sense of safety, my anchor, and my belief in life. The house, once filled with laughter and my mother's comforting presence became a silent place of survival.

I left home for Chandigarh in search of a job, some stability, and a shred of peace. At that time, I didn't know how to handle the grief or the responsibilities entrusted to me. Through a friend's recommendation, I went to a consultant, hoping to find work. But instead of guidance, I walked into a trap. The family who claimed to help me used me instead, making me work long, endless hours. I taught their daughter, and made calls for their business, yet I was paid only ₹500 for each successful placement. Their business thrived on lies, and I couldn't bring myself to deceive people for money. At the end of the month, I earned a mere ₹1500, barely enough to survive.

It was on one of those dark days that I sat on that cold bench, waiting for a school friend who had promised to meet me. I had no money for the next month's PG rent, no food, no job prospects, and no hope. I saw people coming out of cafes and shops, spending money, walking hand in hand with their loved ones some girls with their mothers, too. I remembered my conversations with my mother about becoming successful, buying her a car, and going on road trips. My dreams knew no limits then, and now here I was crying alone, uncertain where my life was taking me.

In the middle of my silent sobs, something unexpected happened. I noticed a foreigner struggling to communicate with someone. Forgetting my pain for a moment, I stood up, walked over, and helped her find what she was looking for. That's who I've always been someone who forgets her own suffering when she sees someone else in need. As I walked back to that bench, a thought struck me: I may not have qualifications or special skills, but I had one thing the ability to communicate.

With my phone battery draining, I quickly searched online, desperate to find something I could do with my limited skills. That's when I saw, an ad that read: Become an IELTS Trainer. I had no idea what IELTS was, but something in me decided then and there that I would give it a shot. I promised myself I'd show up for the interview, no matter what. The next day, I went to an institute called StoneTouch, took the interview, and was invited back for a test. And just like that, I got the job. The salary was ₹15,500 more than I could have imagined at the time. For the first time in months, I felt hope.

Life didn't get easy overnight, but it started to move forward. During orientation at StoneTouch, the owner shared his success story, and as I listened, words began to flow in me like they hadn't in so long. I scribbled down a poem about his journey. A kind girl named Prabhjot, who sat beside me, saw what I had written and raised her hand. "Sir, she's written something about StoneTouch," she said. I froze in shock, her selflessness felt like a rarity in such a competitive world. The owner read my poem, smiled, and loved it. That day, my words made their way to the reception desk of every branch of StoneTouch, framed for everyone to see.

At that moment, I realized something; I wanted to be a writer. I wanted to share my story, my struggles, my pain, and my triumphs with the world. I didn't know how it would happen or when, but the dream was planted deep inside me. Through heartbreaks, disappointments, and years of working tirelessly to survive, that dream lived quietly in me.

I began to manifest this dream with everything I had, sitting for hours imagining my book cover, the title shining bright and my name on it. I visualized my life as a writer, the joy of holding my first book, and people knowing my name. Every single day, I meditated on these moments. I would close my eyes and see myself writing, my pen gliding across the pages, my words touching hearts. I lived this dream in my mind before it became my reality. Today, as I write this chapter, I realize I have become the writer I always dreamed of being. My first book is coming soon, and this moment feels surreal. The universe has finally rewarded the faith I had in my vision.

This journey taught me that life gives us glimmers of hope, even in our darkest moments. The bench in Sector 17 was not just a place of despair; it became the moment where my life began to turn, and I started to manifest a new reality. I learned that dreams survive only when we refuse to let go, even when the world seems to conspire against us.

Manifestation is about belief, persistence, and action no matter how small the steps. From sitting on that lonely bench to writing this chapter, I have realized that the universe rewards those who dare to dream again.

## About the Author

I am Ruchika Bhasker, a passionate writer, a data analyst by profession, and a believer in the power of manifestation. Having faced loss, struggle, and hopelessness, I transformed my pain into purpose and words. Through this chapter, I hope to inspire others to trust their dreams, no matter how distant they may seem. My journey is proof that even the darkest days hold the light of new beginnings.

# BAKING MY DREAM INTO A REALITY

## BY MADHURI PREMNATH

## Introduction

It was 12 pm on a Friday, my cupcake bakery was busy with walk-ins and order pickups for the weekend. The phone rang and I answered with pride and humility gushing out at the same time, the young lady on the other end politely asked me, "Do you cater to wedding orders? I love your cupcakes and would love to have them at my wedding instead of a wedding cake." My eyes lit up and with a big smile on my face and an affirmative nod. I replied, "Of course we do and I would love to help you."

How did I get here? How did this happen? Was it a dream or reality?

It had been only 4 months since the opening of my bake shop and I received my first big order and was simply ecstatic. The dream of owning my very own cupcake shop was finally a reality and the genuine love and feedback that I was receiving every day made me feel warm and happy. My heart was full.

## The Desire and the Journey

I started as a home baker like everyone else, baking with boxed mixes and experimenting with different flavours. In the course of time, I realized that I absolutely love the art and science of baking, it became my therapy and my go-to space to unwind. When I was happy, I would bake, when I was sad, I would bake and the more I baked, the deeper I dived into the process. Besides, I loved cupcakes, unlike a cake, it is the perfect size, visually more eye-catching and fun for all ages and I started learning more about the art of baking cupcakes and making them unique and different from everything that was available out there. The desire to be uncommon and one of a kind with my recipes, presentation and taste drove me to be innovative in my approach. I started dreaming of owning my very own bake shop one day.

I was still working my IT job and the idea of owning a cupcake shop and implementing it as a business seemed far-fetched. One day, my friend narrated the story of the deaf frog to me, (On a sunny day, a group of frogs decided to have a race to the top of the mud hill, as the frogs hopped up, they passed comments to distract each other and slow each other down, but there was one deaf frog who could not hear anything and charged up the hill and won the race cause he did not get disturbed by any of the negative comments). Hence, I became the deaf frog and decided to build my dream bakery.

As I focused on my dream project, I carefully curated the steps to master my passion. A year of formal education and a year of running a test kitchen helped me gain confidence in making the best cupcakes.

## The Manifestation Process

I realized that when you are truly passionate about something and love it with all your heart and have a genuine intent, you will give it your best effort and be the best in your endeavour. This thought in all its glory settled deep in my subconscious and gave me the drive and belief to move forward.

As a person who loves to read about wisdom and philosophy, I remembered the words of Lao Tzu, "The Journey of a thousand miles begins with a single step". It was these words that kept me going every day, I took 9 months to curate my menus, recipes, branding, logos and more just like how a mother holds her baby in her womb for 9 months. There were days I was tired and wanted to give up, there were disasters in my kitchen and it felt like everything was going wrong, it was a simple reminder that I needed a break and the next day, I woke up and continued.

At the end of 9 months, I was driving by main street and found my dream location for the bakery, could not believe how everything fell into place step by step. After 2 months of renovation, we opened our doors on a crisp spring morning.

The basis of my manifestation process is that "whatever the mind can conceive and believe, it can achieve". The tools of affirmations, gratitude, persistence and beliefs play a key role in what we manifest.

## Conclusion and Lessons Learned

This experience showed me that true manifestation goes beyond mere wishes, it's about harmonizing our authentic and true intentions with the flow of the universe through trust, gratitude and meaningful action. It gave me validation and understanding that when our desires are authentic and true to ourselves and everyone around us, the steps to fulfilment often appear as if by divine design.

In less than 2 years, my bakery was awarded the best bake shop in the county, I was invited as a judge in a baking competition and the icing on the cupcake, some of my clients became my best friends and close connections for life.

However, I have to say that the biggest lesson has been my personal growth as an individual – learning to embrace challenges, adapt to change, trust my instincts and develop the resilience and passion needed to turn dreams into reality.

## About the Author

"Life is all about unfolding the perfectly imperfect self".

I am an Author, Pastry Chef, Consultant/SME in People & Culture/HRM and Organizational Behaviour.

Published my first e-book on Amazon in April 2023. "A Bottle of Emotions: 5 Reasons to Break the Bottle and Live Life". Received the Amazon #1 Best Seller by May 2023 and International Best Seller by November 2023.

A Bottle of Emotions is a journey of self-discovery to understand how emotions, feelings, and thoughts are vital to understanding who we are.

Successfully owned and operated Bake Shops in Bergen County and Essex County for 5 years. As the of Founder of Baked in a Cup, I conceptualized the Bake Shop from scratch with curated menus and customized offerings. Recognized by Bergen Record as the top 5 Bake shops in Bergen County.

# FROM FEAR TO MIRACLES: A JOURNEY OF FAITH, HEALING, AND MANIFESTATION

## BY SWATI SHARRMA

### Introduction

Two years ago, my life took a dramatic turn when I faced two of the biggest challenges of my life—saving my father's life and creating my dream business. Both journeys tested my strength, faith, and belief in the power of manifestation. Little did I know, that these moments of despair would become milestones of transformation, teaching me that miracles are real and possible. This is the story of how I aligned with the universe and witnessed the impossible becoming reality.

## The Desire and the Journey

### A Father's Life at Stake

My father was diagnosed with a severe heart condition, and doctors declared that his survival chances during surgery were minimal. His heart valve needed to be transplanted, and complications were extremely high. The cost of the procedure was a staggering 35 lakhs, a sum that seemed impossible to arrange. To add to the emotional turmoil, my father strictly instructed, "Do not ask anyone for money. If you do, I won't undergo the surgery."

The pressure was immense, but I refused to give up. I knew I had to manifest this money without seeking external help or taking loans. I turned to the practices I trusted—visualization, journaling, affirmations, gratitude techniques, and chanting powerful mantras. Every morning, I visualized my father recovering, the money flowing effortlessly, and the surgery being successful. I wrote affirmations such as, "I am capable of manifesting abundance to save my father's life," and practiced gratitude for the healing energies already at work.

Then, the universe began aligning in miraculous ways. Mystically, we received a very good offer for a piece of land we owned, which was sold just in time. At the same time, our insurance claim covered 90% of the surgery expenses. It felt like a divine intervention. All the medical tests—3D echo, CT scan, angiography—came through with manageable results. I meditated daily, focusing healing energy on my father and chanting mantras to enhance his recovery.

The critical TAVI process for valve implantation was performed, and two stents were placed during surgery. Despite all odds, the operation was a success. I witnessed miracles unfolding before my eyes, reaffirming my belief in the power of faith and manifestation. My father's recovery was nothing short of a divine blessing, and I emerged from this experience with a renewed sense of purpose and resilience.

## Building a Dream Business in Two Weeks

Soon after my father's recovery, I found myself yearning to create something meaningful—a business that aligned with my passion for holistic healing. I envisioned a venture centred around Seven Chakra Crystals and Essential Oils, combining ancient wisdom with modern needs.

With only two weeks in hand, I started by scripting my dream business as though it was already flourishing. I wrote down every detail: the products, the customers, and the joy of creating a positive impact. I practiced gratitude, thanking the universe for bringing this vision to life. Networking opportunities appeared out of nowhere, and I met people who supported my idea. Orders began pouring in even before the official launch.

The business took off faster than I imagined, and today, it stands as a testament to the fact that dreams backed by faith and action can become reality. My venture has not only brought financial independence but also a deeper sense of fulfilment knowing I am contributing to others' well-being.

## Manifestation Process

The journey of manifesting both these miracles was deeply transformational. Here's what worked for me:

- **Visualization:** I created vivid mental images of my father recovering and my business thriving.
- **Journaling:** Writing down my intentions helped me gain clarity and stay focused.
- **Affirmations:** Positive affirmations like "I am divinely supported" kept my faith strong.
- **Gratitude:** Practicing gratitude for every small blessing amplified the energy of abundance.
- **Meditation and Mantras:** Daily meditation and chanting powerful mantras strengthened my inner peace and belief.

Through these practices, I realized that the universe responds to clarity, faith, and aligned action. Moments of doubt did creep in, but I used these techniques to centre myself and stay connected to the bigger picture.

## Conclusion and Lessons Learned

This journey taught me that miracles are possible when we trust the process of manifestation. It's not just about wishing but about aligning our energy, taking inspired action, and believing in the unseen. Watching my father recover and building my dream business were not just achievements but profound spiritual experiences that deepened my faith in life's infinite possibilities.

To anyone reading this, know that you have the power to manifest your dreams and overcome life's biggest challenges. Trust in your vision, and let the universe guide the way.

## About the Author

I am Swati Sharrma, a corporate professional, mindset healing coach, author, and passionate believer in the transformative power of manifestation and holistic living. Having experienced life-changing miracles firsthand, I am dedicated to helping others unlock their true potential and lead meaningful, empowered lives. Connect with me at www.swatisharrma.com to explore my journey and services.

# THE POWER OF MY "WHY"

### THE DRIVE BEHIND EVERY STEP FORWARD

### BY TAYYABA FATIMA

## Introduction

*"The smallest spark can ignite a flame that transforms a lifetime."*

As a child, I was the youngest of nine siblings, surrounded by a family where roles and responsibilities flowed effortlessly among my elders. I was often shielded from decisions and challenges, living in the secure shadow of my parents. My mother catered to every materialistic need, while my father nurtured our spiritual growth with daily evening wisdom sessions. Yet, my childhood was marked by a lack of personal agency. Friends were confined to the walls of school, and my cousins were too old to relate to my world. Little did I know, this sheltered upbringing would mould the foundation of my biggest transformation. My story is one of rediscovering self-worth and purpose—a journey where my father's guidance planted the seeds of my resilience and ambition.

---

## The Desire and the Journey

Growing up, I never questioned my life's direction. My father was my superhero, and I followed his decisions without hesitation. When the time came for marriage, I stepped into my new life carrying everything my father had given me—from material possessions to a strong moral compass. I didn't know who I truly was or what I wanted beyond fulfilling the roles life handed me. For years, I navigated my new family, facing challenges without ever questioning my own identity.

The turning point arrived unexpectedly after the birth of my youngest son. On the way home from the hospital, my father informed me that he had arranged an interview for me at a school the next day. My initial reaction was simple: "Jo father kahenge, wo karoongi" (I will do whatever my father says). Despite my lack of preparation and confidence, I attended the interview, to face failure. However, with someone's recommendation, I was offered a position. It was at that moment that a new chapter of my life began.

That first job was a seedling of opportunity that grew with time. Year after year, I climbed the ladder—from teacher to assembly in-charge, to Head of Department, and eventually to principal. Along the way, I faced countless challenges. There were moments of doubt, exhaustion, and feeling overwhelmed, but I persisted. My father's faith in my abilities gave me the strength to overcome these hurdles, and each small success added to my confidence.

---

## The Manifestation Process

My journey of transformation wasn't just about external achievements; it was about redefining my inner narrative. As I navigated the challenges of balancing family and career, I began to lean into the power of manifestation. I practiced gratitude for the opportunities that came my way and started visualizing the life I wanted. Every morning, I would set intentions for the day, imagining myself as a confident leader and a source of inspiration for others.

Journaling became a key practice, helping me reflect on my growth and articulate my dreams. Each time I wrote about a goal, I noticed how Allah seemed to conspire in my favour. Serendipitous events, like a recommendation for a promotion or an encouraging word from a colleague, began aligning to propel me forward.

The pivotal realization came when I started believing in my own "Why"—the purpose that fuelled my actions. I understood that my father's guidance wasn't just about following his footsteps; it was about discovering my unique path. The values and lessons he imparted became the foundation of my success, but it was my persistence and belief that turned them into reality.

---

## Conclusion and Lessons Learned

This journey taught me that manifestation is not merely about dreaming but about aligning with purpose through faith, gratitude, and inspired action. It's about turning obstacles into stepping stones and trusting the process even when the path seems unclear. My "Why"—the desire to honour my father's legacy while discovering my own potential—transformed my life. From a timid girl living in her family's shadow, I became an international author, founder of a school, and a guide to others seeking their purpose.

Manifestation is not magic; it's a practice of intentional living. When we clarify our desires and persist with our beliefs, Allah aligns us in miraculous ways to reveal our true potential.

---

## About the Author

I am Tayyaba Fatima, an international author, educator, and founder of a successful school. With over 20 years of experience in education, I have received multiple awards, including Best Teacher and Best Principal. My journey of manifestation has been a testament to the power of resilience, faith, and purpose. Through my work, I strive to inspire others to discover their own "Why" and create lives filled with meaning and success.

# FROM CHAOS TO CLARITY: MANIFESTING MY LIFE PURPOSE

## BY ANAND IYER

*I*t was July 2023, and my life was at a crossroads. I had just left behind a stable job, stepping into the unknown with nothing but a dream and the hope of creating something meaningful. The dream was deeply personal—a culmination of years of experience and a burning desire to make an impact.

But then, disaster struck. A freak accident in my bathroom left me with a fractured wrist. Being right-handed, this injury halted my plans entirely. Daily tasks became painfully challenging, and my once-clear vision of the future began to blur.

As if the physical pain wasn't enough, financial pressures began mounting. The severance package I had relied upon dwindled rapidly, and legal troubles stemming from my role as a secretary in my housing society piled on. Police summons, court battles and sleepless nights consumed me.

I felt trapped, with no way forward and no way back. In this despair, I discovered **Ho'oponopono**, an ancient Hawaiian technique for clearing negativity and restoring harmony. At first, it seemed too simple to be effective, but I was desperate enough to try anything.

## The Desire and the Journey

This journey wasn't just about survival—it was about purpose. Deep down, I knew I wanted to create something that would matter to myself and others. Yet, the obstacles I faced made me question everything.

As I began practising Ho'oponopono, repeating the phrases *"I am sorry, Please forgive me, Thank you, and I love you,"* I started noticing subtle shifts in my mindset. Slowly, clarity began to return. One day, during a meditation session, a story from my past came to mind: **"Acres of Diamonds."**

## The Story of Acres of Diamonds

Ali Hafed, a prosperous farmer, lived contentedly by the River Indus. One day, a wise man told him of diamonds—precious stones so valuable that even one could make a person immensely wealthy.

That night, Ali Hafed couldn't sleep. The thought of finding diamonds consumed him. He decided to sell his farm and search the world for these treasures. For years, he wandered far and wide, spending his wealth and chasing a dream that always seemed just out of reach.

In the end, penniless and broken, Ali Hafed died in despair, never finding the diamonds he sought.

The man who purchased the property noticed something sparkling in the stream on his old farm. To his amazement, it was a diamond. Further exploration revealed that the entire farm sat on one of the richest diamond mines ever discovered.

## The Turning Point

This story hit me like a bolt of lightning. I realized I had been searching outward for solutions when the answers I needed were within me all along. Like Ali Hafed, I had overlooked my "acres of diamonds."

Through Ho'oponopono, I began to uncover the treasures in my life. My passions—technology, writing, real estate, and fitness—have always been with me. Still, none felt like the ultimate purpose I was seeking. Then, one day, I had a breakthrough.

I looked at my name, Anand Iyer, in a new light and saw the letters "AI." It was a moment of profound clarity. Artificial Intelligence wasn't just a fascination; it was my calling. Its potential to transform lives aligned perfectly with my dream of creating something impactful.

## Manifesting My Vision

With this newfound clarity, I committed myself to empowering 1 Billion people worldwide by leveraging AI. My focus became helping small and medium businesses thrive and enabling professionals and women on career breaks to create financial freedom through multiple income streams.

I developed a framework called **AI R.I.C.H.E.S**, which provides practical steps for applying AI to transform lives:

**R** – Recognize Opportunities with AI- Spot AI-driven growth areas in your industry.

**I** – Invest in Learning- Build essential skills to harness AI

**C** – Create Value- Use AI tools to solve real-world problems

**H** – Harness Productivity- Automate tasks for maximum efficiency

**E** – Establish Multiple Income Streams- Leverage AI for freelancing and consulting

**S** – Secure Financial Freedom- Build sustainable income and reclaim your time

I also began writing a book series or a "Book Flix" to demystify AI and make it accessible to everyone. Opportunities began flowing in as clients resonated with my vision. For the first time, I felt aligned with my purpose.

## Lessons from Acres of Diamonds

Reflecting on the story of Ali Hafed, I discovered profound truths that changed my life:

1. **Your Treasure Lies Within You**
   Like Ali Hafed's farm, our most incredible resources are often right before us. Recognizing and nurturing these treasures is the first step to fulfilment.
2. **Shift Your Perspective**
   What we dismiss as ordinary may hold extraordinary potential. Changing how we view our circumstances often reveals hidden opportunities. Also, the darkest times in your life are the gateway to hidden and new opportunities.
3. **Contentment and Gratitude**
   True wealth begins with appreciating what you already have. Gratitude transforms challenges into stepping stones for growth.

### 4. Clarity and Alignment

Ali Hafed's downfall was a lack of clarity. Manifestation requires aligning your goals with your inner values to unlock your true purpose.

## Conclusion

This journey taught me that the answers we seek are often closer than we think. By clearing negativity, embracing gratitude, and trusting the process, we can manifest a life of abundance and purpose.

To anyone reading this, remember: your "acres of diamonds" lie within you. Look inward, nurture your gifts, and trust the universe to guide you toward your destiny.

---

## About the Author

Anand Iyer is a seasoned IT professional and an AI Coach and Consultant turned entrepreneur with over two decades of experience in IT, specifically in Digital Transformation and Artificial Intelligence. As an author, coach, and AI Evangelist for personal growth, he specializes in using manifestation techniques like Ho'oponopono and the power of Artificial Intelligence (AI) to help individuals and businesses unlock their potential and achieve lasting success.

# MANIFESTATIONS, THE UNIVERSE STAMPING

## BY NAZNEEN ZEESHAN ALI

*T*his chapter explores three pivotal manifestations in my life, each of which shaped my journey in profound ways: building mud houses, admiring a well-dressed professor, and becoming a world-renowned author.

### The First Manifestation: Building Mud Houses and Becoming a Builder

As a child, I spent countless hours in the yard of our home, moulding small structures out of mud and dirt

I would spend hours perfecting these tiny homes and imagined myself as the builder, designing communities. At the time, I didn't know the word "manifestation," but I can now see that in my innocent yet focused repetition, I was envisioning a future where I, too, would construct buildings on a grander scale.

Years later, as I pursued my studies and entered the field of construction, I began to realize that this early childhood play was not mere fantasy. It was the beginning of a profound connection to construction, to design, and to the very act of shaping spaces that would house people and ideas. I could trace the lineage of my career directly back to those days of building with mud.

They were the foundation – quite literally – of my journey as a builder. Today, I manage my own firm, constructing buildings that house communities and businesses. And whenever I plan a new project site, I smile to myself, thinking back to those childhood moments when I first "manifested" the life I now live.

## The Second Manifestation: Admiring a Professor and Becoming Financially Successful

During my time at college, there was one professor who stood out among all others – a lady who was not only intellectually brilliant but also impeccably dressed, confident, and financially successful. Her well-wrapped sarees, heeled bellies, and air of authority were magnetic, but it wasn't just her appearance that drew me in.

I remember, vividly, sitting in her lectures, hanging on every word as she discussed topics that were far beyond the textbook. To me, she embodied the ultimate version of success – the balance of intelligence, wealth, and style.

In those days, I made a silent vow to myself: I would one day be as smart, as well-dressed, and as financially prosperous as she was. It wasn't just about the money, but about the lifestyle and freedom it represented. I began to visualize myself not only excelling in my career but also achieving the kind of financial success that would afford me the luxuries of life that this professor seemed to effortlessly enjoy.

Fast forward a decade, and I find myself at the helm of a successful business venture. My financial portfolio is thriving, and I live a life that combines my professional passions with the wealth and confidence I had once admired in my professor. And, while I may not have realized it in those early years, the admiration I felt for that professor was not just about wanting her lifestyle – it was the manifestation of my own desire to step into that role and create a life of financial freedom and influence.

## The Third Manifestation: Becoming a World-Famous Author

Even as a child, I had an innate love for stories. My imagination was vast, and writing stories became a way for me to express that inner world. But those were just stories written in notes not in a proper book.

In high school, I wrote poetry; in college, short stories. But it wasn't until my late forties, as I grappled with my professional career, that I began to think seriously about writing a book. At first, it felt like a pipe dream — something for authors more successful than I could ever be. But then I remembered something that had always been in the back of my mind: I had always imagined myself becoming a published author, a voice whose words could inspire and connect with others on a global scale.

The idea of becoming a world-famous author had been with me since childhood. I'd daydreamed about signing books at launch events, being interviewed on talk shows, and seeing my work on bestseller lists. I often envisioned my name printed in bold letters on the cover of a book, admired by readers all over the world.

In 2023, I took the plunge and began to write my first book. I set aside time every day, no matter how busy my life became, to write. Slowly, those drafts transformed into a finished manuscript. The book named "Let's Kill the Cancer Before It Kills Us" was published on Amazon, and to my surprise, it gained traction and was recorded in the Limca Book of Records for making a world record (maximum number of eBooks published together by the International Council of Authors by Inspiring Jatin). Readers loved it, and it eventually became a bestseller.

Today, I am a published author of multiple books, with a global readership and recognition in literary circles. I often think back to my childhood, to the dream of becoming an author – a dream that seemed so distant then but is so tangible now. The manifestation of this desire took time, effort, and persistence, but it all started with a small idea, a seed planted in my mind during those early years of scribbling stories in notebooks.

## Conclusion: The Power of Manifestation

The three manifestations I've shared – becoming a builder, achieving financial success, and becoming a world-famous author – didn't happen by accident. They were the result of dreams, both conscious and subconscious, that I nurtured over the years. As a child, I didn't know the term "manifestation," but I now understand that these childhood dreams were the seeds of my adult reality. Each manifestation required focus, action, and the belief that what I envisioned was possible.

Our thoughts and dreams are more powerful than we often realize. By holding onto them, nurturing them, and aligning our actions with our aspirations, we can turn the impossible into the possible. We are all capable of manifesting the life we desire – just as I manifested mine.

# THE POWER OF INTENTION: SETTING THE FOUNDATION FOR MY MANIFESTATION JOURNEY

## BY JYOTI KR ARORAA

*A* year ago, I found myself engulfed in stress, constantly annoyed by the smallest of inconveniences. I felt overwhelmed by the weight of my responsibilities, believing I was doing so much for others while receiving little to no appreciation in return. This unhealthy mindset overthinking culminated in a health scare—chest pain that led me to the emergency room, where I faced the terrifying reality of a heart attack. It was a wake-up call that forced me to reevaluate my life and its meaning.

- In the aftermath of this life-changing experience, I realized the importance of self-care, gratitude, and the power of manifestation. I learnt and practiced various methods of self-care. My journey of transformation began with specific practices and tools that helped realign my focus and intentions. In this, my family is the best support for making me a positive ecosystem.

## Specific Practices and Tools for Manifestation

1. **Visualization**: Every morning, I spend a few minutes visualizing my ideal life. I imagined myself healthy, happy, and fulfilled, which helped me grasp the feeling of achieving my desires.
2. **Journaling**: I kept a manifestation journal, where I documented my goals, dreams, and daily affirmations. This ritual became an anchor in my journey and allowed me to track my progress.
3. **Affirmations**: I created personalized affirmations to reinforce my intentions. Phrases like "I am worthy of love and appreciation", "I am capable of achieving my goals" & " I am Achiever, Achiever" became part of my daily routine.
4. **Gratitude Practice**: Daily gratitude helped shift my mindset from scarcity to abundance. I focused on the

positive aspects of my life, which drew more positivity my way.

5. **Ho'oponopono**: I practiced this Hawaiian technique of forgiveness, which allowed me to release resentment and heal past wounds. Saying "I'm sorry," "Please forgive me," "Thank you," and "I love you" helped create peace within me.

6. **Meditation**: I incorporated meditation into my daily practices, which allowed me to cultivate a sense of calm and clarity. It became a powerful tool for connecting with my inner self and examining my intentions deeply.

7. **Scripting**: I wrote out my goals as if they had already happened, immersing myself in the emotions of success and gratitude for their fulfilment.

8. **Breathing:** Exercises help me to -**Aligning Energy**: calm my mind, focus energy, and create a positive mindset conducive to attracting my desires. Mindful breathing increases self-awareness and introspection, allowing me to recognize limiting beliefs and negative thoughts that hinder my manifestation efforts. Controlled and deep breathing invoke feelings of gratitude, love, and joy, emotions that are powerful in the law of attraction and manifestation processes which helped ground my energy, connecting to the present moment and making it easier to reflect on past experiences and future intentions with more clarity.

## Key Moments of Transformation

With a clear purpose to add value to people's life. I put my full dedication to these practices, I experienced significant transformations over the year. I set ten specific manifestations, of which I achieved three of them, while others are still in progress:

1. **Weight Loss Journey**: One of my primary goals was to lose weight. I focused my intentions on achieving a healthier lifestyle, and through a combination of diet and exercise, I successfully reduced my weight from 110 kg to 79 kg in just six months.
2. **Learning to Swim**: A casual dip in the pool turned into a transformation journey. At 52 years old, I had always dreamed of learning how to swim. I set my manifestation to learn swimming in just eight hours over the course of eight days and I achieved this gracefully, of course, I give Gratitude to all Coaches. Consistently, I swim everyday at 7am. Discipline beat Motivation. Remarkably, I not only achieved this goal but swam continuously 20 laps of 50m, which shifted my mindset and manifested in winning a breaststroke contest.
3. **Waking Up at 5 AM**: In January 2024, I made a resolution to wake up at 5 AM every day for a whole year, regardless of when I went to bed. Joining the 5 AM Club provided the structure and motivation,

I needed, and I not only achieved this goal but also found my productivity and serenity greatly enhanced.

- If my story inspires you connect me to make a positive ecosystem
- What are your manifest /resolutions for which you are dying for?

As I reflect on my journey, I encourage you to ponder your own manifestations and resolutions. What goals are you passionate about? Are you ready to take the steps necessary to bring those desires into reality? Remember, the journey of manifestation begins with clarity of intention and a commitment to taking action. Together, let's unlock the potential within us and create the lives we truly desire. Nurture your gifts, and trust the universe to guide you toward your destiny.

## About the Author

Jyoti Kr Aroraa is an introvert, an esteemed alumnus of the Indian Institute of Foreign Trade, a certified customs broker, and dynamic CEO of "CARGO MOVERS" IATA. With over 25+ years of experience in International logistics, Jyoti has dedicated his career to empowering businesses to scale new heights while achieving significant cost reductions—often saving clients up to 25%.

A passionate mentor, he has guided over 5,000 entrepreneurs on their journeys to success. His leadership roles as an ex-President of BNI and Vice President of Toastmasters highlight his commitment to fostering community and professional development. His mission is to inspire others to harness the power of intention and manifest their dreams into reality

Connect with me-https://www.linkedin.com/in/jyoti-kr-aroraa-6a9a5235/

arora@cargomovers.co.in

https://www.youtube.com/@cargomoversjkaror5254

- Trust this chapter will help you in your life transformation changes

# FROZEN FURY AND UNSHAKEN SPIRIT

## MANIFESTING SAFETY AND STRENGTH IN THE FACE OF A DEADLY BLIZZARD

### BY RUPALI MUKHERJEE

### Introduction

"In the silence of the storm, one must listen to the soul's whispers."

My father, a retired Army officer, has always been the embodiment of strength and resilience. Awarded multiple times for his bravery and leadership during his service, he remains my greatest inspiration. This story is drawn from a real-life experience when he was stationed in Leh, a remote city in Ladakh, Jammu & Kashmir. Leh, with its snow-covered peaks in winter, exudes an untouched beauty during the summer, as the snow gently rests on the mountain tops. I had always dreamed of playing in the snow, so I decided to visit my father there.

What unfolded was an unforgettable experience where the whispers of a raging blizzard were drowned by the power of faith and belief. I vividly remember my father's calming words in the face of nature's fury: "Team, do not worry. This is nature's cry, a reflection of how it has been treated by humankind. If we remain calm and pray for its well-being, it will send us the light of hope."

## The Desire and The Journey

I have always been a travel enthusiast, thanks to my father's transferable job. After finishing my board exams that summer, we planned a trip to Ladakh, where my father was posted as the commanding officer. The thought of seeing snow for the first time filled me with excitement.

We flew from Chandigarh to Leh and stayed in a thick-walled mud house with rooftop windows to acclimatize to the oxygen-deficient environment. After a few days, Dad announced a trip to a cantonment area 100 km north of Leh, crossing the Khardungla Pass at 17,582 ft, the world's highest avalanche bridge. He invited me to join him, and I couldn't wait to experience this adventure.

We began our journey early in the morning. As we climbed higher, the air grew colder, and signs of human habitation became sparse. The Pass was still 10 km away, and we needed to cross it before 1 pm to avoid a dangerous blizzard. However, just as we reached a ridge, Dad's jeep broke down. It was 12:30 pm. He ordered the troop to proceed ahead, leaving the driver and us behind.

Moments later, the blizzard hit with full force. We took shelter in a small temple nearby as the storm raged around us. The winds howled, and snow fell like a relentless curtain, burying everything in sight. The temperature plummeted, and visibility dropped to almost zero. Fear consumed me, but my father's calm demeanour kept me grounded.

"This is nature's power," he said. "Pray and think positively. Nature will return its love if we respect it." His words gave me hope as we huddled together, trying to stay warm.

An hour passed, and the storm began to mellow. Just as despair threatened to take hold, we saw a distant light piercing through the snowfall. A rescue jeep approached from the other side of the Pass. The troop had sent it after realizing our delay. It felt like a miracle as the rescue team helped us out of the storm's clutches.

That day, amidst the wrath of nature, I learned the power of resilience, faith, and calmness in adversity. My father's unwavering belief in the power of positivity had saved us, turning what could have been a tragedy into a lesson in courage and hope.

## The Manifestation Process

Manifestation involves channelling thoughts, emotions, and energies toward a desired outcome, aligning one's inner state with the external reality one seeks to create. It emphasizes the transformative power of focused intention, positivity, and belief, especially in challenging situations.

In this narration, my father serves as a guiding force in initiating the manifestation process during a life-threatening blizzard. Amidst the chaos and fear, his calm and composed demeanour becomes an anchor for positive energy. His instructions to pray and think positive thoughts underscore the importance of maintaining respect and harmony with nature. This reflects the first step of manifestation: **setting a clear and respectful intention.** Rather than succumbing to panic, we focused our thoughts on surviving the storm and seeking help.

The second step is **visualization and belief.** Visualization directs the mind toward desired outcomes, steering it away from fear and despair. As we prayed, my father's unwavering faith inspired a shared belief in rescue and safety. This belief became a mental alignment with the possibility of survival, reinforcing hope and optimism in a seemingly hopeless situation.

A crucial aspect of the manifestation process is **emotional alignment.** My father's calmness instilled a sense of security and resilience in me, despite the terrifying conditions. Negative emotions like fear and despair can obstruct manifestation, but cultivating hope, gratitude, and trust ensures the flow of positive energy. This emotional stability played a vital role in keeping us mentally strong as we braved the storm.

The final step of manifestation is **allowing and receiving.** By maintaining positive intentions and emotional alignment, we opened ourselves to the possibility of rescue. As the storm began to subside, our focus and prayers seemed to harmonize with external reality. The arrival of the rescue jeep felt like a miraculous response to our combined energy and faith.

This experience illustrates the profound connection between inner belief and external reality. Manifestation is not merely wishful thinking; it is a disciplined process of aligning thoughts, emotions, and intentions with a desired outcome. Through calm determination, faith, and emotional alignment, we overcame the wrath of nature, demonstrating how the power of manifestation can turn adversity into triumph.

## Conclusions and Lessons Learned

This deadly incident demonstrates that the mind and spirit can rise above fear to find solutions and hope. It reinforces that manifestation can turn the most challenging situations into opportunities for survival and growth.

**Calmness in Crisis:** My father's composure amidst chaos proved pivotal. Staying calm allows clear thinking and inspires hope in others.

**Power of Positive Thinking:** Focusing on survival, rather than fear, channelled our energies toward a solution. Optimism can turn even the darkest moments into golden opportunities.

**Emotional Alignment:** Fear can cloud judgment but aligning emotions with hope and trust fosters resilience and clarity. Gratitude and faith are essential during crises.

**Respect for Nature:** My father's advice to respect nature teaches that nature is powerful and unpredictable, and humans must approach it with humility and understanding.

**Action and Belief:** Manifestation is not about wishful thinking—it requires a focused intention, emotional alignment, and openness to outcomes.

## About the Author

I, Rupali Mukherjee, a Physics postgraduate, am a passionate educationist with over two decades of teaching experience. I have dedicated my career to teaching Science and designing innovative curricula that connect learning with everyday life. Honoured with awards like Best Science Teacher (State and National levels), I have guided countless students to manifest their potential and achieve their dreams.

I firmly believe in the power of manifestation—aligning thoughts, actions, and beliefs to transform aspirations into reality. I hope my story inspires others to harness this power in their lives.

# MAGIC CANVAS OF A SCHOOLGIRL: A LIFE WELL-LIVED

## BY SWAPNIL ROY 'SOULTINKER

*(Dedicated to my parents, for raising me to believe that anything is possible!)*

**Introduction:** When I was a schoolgirl, a teacher asked us to write an essay on "If life were a painting and you were the artist, what would you paint?" This sparked my manifestation journey. I wrote that essay, and what I wrote still gives me hope and beauty, like magic glasses to see life joyously!

Now in my forties, I sometimes feel anxious about having lived half my life, but I'm also satisfied with my heartfelt memories. That high school activity inspired me to create and pursue the life I desire.

**The Desire and the Journey:** Here's the excerpt from those torn pages, still with me:

*"If life were a painting, I would depict a beautiful mountain river flowing over rounded pebbles and scattered rocks, amidst a lush green forest. I'd be sitting on one of those rocks, enjoying the mild sunshine, with my feet dipped into the cold, clear stream. I envision myself joyous, lively, and full of hope, absorbing nature's unparalleled beauty. The river would glisten in the golden sunlight, flowing with its relaxing sound. Distant bird chirps as my heart's music.*

*My life's canvas is clear as I write about it. The sky is light blue with golden sunlight shimmer. I'm wearing a comfortable white floral dress, and my light brown hair flows freely in the wind. The boldest colour would be forest green, signifying my blissful connection to nature.*

*My painting would be a personal masterpiece, bringing tranquillity and joy whenever I glimpse it, safe from outside opinions. It would reflect my emotions of love and joy, memories of laughter, and human connections with family, friends, and even strangers. I'd feel blissful remembering the loving souls I encountered in my journey.*

*If others saw it, I hope they'd feel life's beauty, making their worries melt away. The serene beauty of nature, with a hint of wilderness, would surface. My life, as a painting on the blessed canvas, would evoke joy and tranquillity in that very moment.*

**The Manifestation:** Since that day and that essay, I gained a new outlook on life. I realized I was born to live a blissful life, no matter what. Writing out my thoughts gave me clarity and a vision of what resonated with me. I wanted to rewrite my story based on my painting. I no longer believed in the idea that happiness was contingent on achieving certain milestones. I felt joy and hope, knowing I was here to experience the beauty of life and learn from human emotions.

I came to understand that life is part of a long soul journey. Each person I met contributed to my collection of beautiful memories and insightful lessons. I embraced life with minimal inhibitions and high hopes. I never craved luxury but cherished the moments spent in nature. I gave my best to practical matters, viewing them as stepping stones to a higher vision of bliss and satisfaction amidst nature.

My passion for traveling and love for reading and writing began in childhood and grew over time. Eventually, I authored a few bestsellers. The canvas I painted as a schoolgirl inspired me to explore nature and pursue my dreams. Alongside practical responsibilities, I found a life partner who walks hand-in-hand with me through life. My life filled with the colours I chose, supported by family, friends, colleagues, and even strangers who enriched my journey.

I worked in organizations that aligned with my hidden aspirations, always making informed decisions that brought clarity and peace of mind. Though life wasn't perfect, the imperfections added fun and adventure, enriching the hues of my life's painting. I manifested a beautiful life, filled with joy, learning, and connection.

**Conclusion:** I am full of gratitude for everything that crossed my path, loving life more each day. I embrace struggles as they add depth to life and offer lasting lessons. I feel blessed, a rarity when many are unhappy over trivial matters. Sometimes I uplift them, but often it's best to let them find their own path and learn. I firmly believe in visualizing a perfect life.

I love journaling to gain clarity, often writing about life's hidden beauty, even in seemingly unfavourable situations. Nature's ways of reviving us from any catastrophe fascinate me, and I believe time heals everything. I habitually affirm positive thoughts to myself, which I later learned are called 'affirmations,' and they certainly help in daily life.

## About the Author

The author **Ms. Swapnil Roy 'Soultinker'** embraces life with frankness and cheerfulness, cherishing her role as a mother of two lively children. She values sincerity in relationships and enjoys hobbies like reading, music, traveling, and gardening, embodying typical Aries traits. With degrees in Mechanical Engineering and Business Administration (specialisation in Human Resource), she has diverse work experience across sectors. She continues working in an office while writing books in her spare time, blending wit, humour, and practical insights in her works.

# CONCLUSION: EMBRACING THE POWER OF MANIFESTATION

*A*s you turn the final pages of this anthology, pause for a moment. Close your eyes. Take a deep breath. Reflect on everything you've just read. What emotions rise within you? What moments from these stories resonate with your own life? Have you seen glimpses of yourself in the struggles and triumphs of these authors?

Manifestation is more than just an idea—it is a way of shaping reality. But reading about it is not enough. **Now is the time to take action.** Grab a journal, a notepad, or even the blank pages of this book and write down what you have discovered about yourself through these stories.

- **What limiting beliefs have held you back?**
- **What dreams have you put on hold, thinking they were impossible?**
- **What is one area of your life where you are ready to manifest something greater?**

Write it down. Make it real. The first step to transformation is acknowledging where you are and deciding where you want to go.

## Your Manifestation Journey Begins Now

This book was never meant to be just an anthology—it is a catalyst for change. If there is one message I hope you take away, it is this: **you are the creator of your reality.** The power to shape your future has always been within you. It is time to harness it.

Here's what to do next:

1. **Define Your Vision Clearly:** Write down exactly what you want to manifest, in as much detail as possible.
2. **Align Your Thoughts and Actions:** Every single day, take intentional steps toward your goal.
3. **Embrace Gratitude:** Be grateful for what you have while welcoming the abundance that is on its way.
4. **Trust the Process:** The universe operates on divine timing—be patient, stay committed, and have faith.
5. **Stay Open to Possibilities:** Manifestation often works in ways you least expect. Stay open to synchronicities and new opportunities.

This is not just about hoping—it is about **believing, aligning, and acting.**

Conclusion: Embracing the Power of Manifestation

Before you close this book, take one more step. **Write down three things you are ready to manifest in your life.** Commit to them. Keep them visible. Let them be a constant reminder that your future is yours to create.

Thank you for being part of this journey. May you move forward with renewed belief, limitless potential, and the courage to manifest the life of your dreams.

# JOIN THE MOVEMENT: SHARE YOUR MANIFESTATION GOALS!

*Y*our journey doesn't end here—it begins now. The stories in this book are powerful, but YOUR story is just as important. Let's inspire others to take action!

- **Post the first 3 things you want to manifest** after learning the techniques in this book on your **Instagram Story** and tag **@inspiringjatin**.
- If you are reading the **paperback version**, take a picture with your copy of the book and share it on your **Instagram Story**, tagging **@inspiringjatin**.

By sharing, you're not only committing to your manifestations but also inspiring others to start their journey. Let's create a wave of transformation together!

**Tag @inspiringjatin & Let the Universe Work Its Magic!** ✨

# YOUR STORY DESERVES TO BE TOLD– BECOME A SELF PUBLISHED AUTHOR!

*H*ave you ever felt a deep desire to share your story, your knowledge, or your life lessons with the world? Perhaps you've imagined holding your own book in your hands, but doubts have held you back—questions like, *Do I have enough experience? Where do I even begin? Will anyone want to read what I write?*

Here's the truth: **Every person has a story worth sharing, including you.** You don't need to be a seasoned writer or an expert in publishing. What you need is the willingness to take the first step.

Becoming a self-published author is one of the most powerful ways to establish **credibility**, **impact lives**, and create a lasting **legacy**. Imagine the feeling of seeing your name on the cover of a book, knowing that your words are inspiring, educating, and transforming others. **That's the power of authorship!**

## But How Do You Get Started?

This is where guidance makes all the difference.

I, **Inspiring Jatin,** have helped thousands of individuals—just like you—become self published bestselling authors without prior writing experience. Through my **Bestselling Author Mastery Workshop**, I take aspiring authors through a step-by-step process to write, publish, and market their books successfully.

You don't need to figure it all out on your own. You just need a proven roadmap and a mentor who has walked the path before you. **And I am here to help.**

## Ready to Take the First Step?

☐ **Scan the QR Code below to register for my Bestselling Author Mastery Workshop and start your journey to becoming a published author.**

**Your story matters. Your voice deserves to be heard. Let's make it happen together!**

www.ingramcontent.com/pod-product-compliance
Lightning Source LLC
LaVergne TN
LVHW041932070526
838199LV00051BA/2780

*9789367071588*